DAVID G. BRADLEY is Associate Professor of Religion at Duke University. He holds degrees from the University of Southern California, Garrett Seminary, and Northwestern University, and received the Ph.D. from Yale in biblical studies. In the last ten years Professor Bradley has shifted his scholarly interest from the Bible and Christian thought to the religions of Asia. In 1955 he studied at the School of Oriental and African Studies of the University of London learning Sanskrit and reading in Hindu and Buddhist history and philosophy.

A Guide to the

WORLD'S RELIGIONS

David G. Bradley

PRENTICE-HALL, INC.

Englewood Cliffs, N. J.

To My Mother and Father

PREFACE

With secularism, nationalism, communism, and other movements making increasing bids for the loyalties of man, the responsible citizen is confronted most forcibly with the need to understand his own religious loyalties, as well as those of his neighbors. Many questions about the world's religions could be discussed at great length. Why are Judaism and Hinduism today essentially cultural expressions, whereas Buddhism, Christianity, and Islam have become world faiths? Is the ethical concern of the Buddhist, the Christian, or the Communist really the same concern, or do the basic presuppositions of each result in a different evaluation of the worth of man and of the manner in which he should be treated? Is there actually a different god for each religion, or is there one god that all religions worship differently? Is it possible to know the real nature of man, considering how varied are the views held by the different religions?

These and similar questions, although not discussed explicitly in this book, underlie any meaningful study of religion. But before such questions can be asked intelligently and discussed with any degree of confidence, it is necessary to have the basic facts available in some manageable form.

This book is intended to introduce the reader to the major contemporary religions. No attempt is made to break new ground, but rather to summarize accurately the essential teaching for each faith concerning salvation. Such a guidebook as this is in no way a substitute for reading the sacred writings of the great religions, nor does it pretend to offer a detailed analysis of the metaphysical systems and rival philosophies which the different religions have produced. For any thorough knowledge of man's religions, one should be familiar with their founders, their basic scriptures, and their mystical and devotional literature. The reader is urged to use the increasing number of excellent introductions and discussions that are now available in paperback form. A selective bibliography of paperbounds on the history of religions is given at the end of this volume.

I would like here to thank the Duke University Research Council for their interest and support in furnishing funds for the typing of this manuscript. I owe a special debt of gratitude to my colleague, Dr. Herbert Patrick Sullivan, who read the entire manuscript and made numerous suggestions for improvement of style and clarification of fact and meaning, and also to his wife, Jo, whose comments on form and style were most helpful. I have also been fortunate in having as typist Mrs. Jacob Kaplan, whose accuracy is remarkable and who aided me with thoughtful questions far beyond the call of duty.

D. G. B.

TABLE OF CONTENTS

INTRODUCTION   1

Part One

THE RELIGION OF PRIMITIVE PEOPLES

ONE   Man and Religion   6

TWO   The Religion of Primitive Peoples   12

Part Two

THE RELIGIONS OF BIBLICAL LANDS

THREE   The Ancient Near East   20

FOUR   Judaism   24

FIVE   Zoroastrianism   39

SIX   Christianity   46

SEVEN   Islam   67

Part Three

THE RELIGIONS OF INDIA

EIGHT   The Land of India   81

NINE   Hinduism   85

TEN   Jainism   103

ELEVEN   Buddhism   108

TWELVE   Sikhism   125

ix

Part Four

THE RELIGIONS OF CHINA AND JAPAN

THIRTEEN   The Origins of Chinese Religion   131

FOURTEEN   Taoism   134

FIFTEEN   Confucianism   141

SIXTEEN   Shinto   150

A Bibliography of Paperbound Books   157

Index   177

INTRODUCTION

The study of religions involves such varied disciplines as history, ethnology, linguistics, literature, sociology, and philosophy, as well as the actual religious thought and practice of all religions. Over the past century intensive scholarship has accumulated a vast and unwieldy amount of information in this field. Our task, therefore, is to organize these data, combining and relating the crucial points.

Man's religions and their scriptures inevitably reflect human experience, whatever their claim to supernatural revelation. This explains the extensive repetition and similarity to be found in the teaching and practice of the various religions. For each religion addresses itself to man's basic concerns about the meaning of life. All religions have world views which can be presented under such rubrics as the world of the spirit, the nature of man, salvation, and destiny.

But such an approach is sterile unless another consideration is kept uppermost. If all religions actually not only are similar in concern but also have no significant or irreconcilable differences, it is likely that agreement between religions would have been arrived at long since. In fact, however, each of the three main groups of religions—those arising in biblical lands, in India, and in East Asia—presupposes widely differing views of these same crucial human concerns.

There are parallels to this lack of agreement in other areas of human relations. The political structure of some societies is monarchical, with a nobility and commoners; others are ruled by a dictatorship. Some societies follow a democratic form of government and others are under communist rule. Although each is composed of human beings with similar passions, hopes, and fears, few would argue that it makes no difference whether one lives under the Russian brand of communism or in a democracy. Again, in the field of economics, whether one examines a bartering society, a capitalistic structure, or a socialistic economy, it is obvious that each is a human society. But differences between these forms of economic organization are also apparent. The similarities between such societies are far greater than the differences, yet it is the differences which help us to understand the meaning and significance of each. And these differences are found especially in the presuppositions which underlie the political or economic theory of a given human society. The "divine right of kings," the "dictatorship of the proletariat," "vox populi, vox dei," "from each according to his ability, to each according to his need," and other basic assumptions come easily to mind.

In the same vein the uniqueness of a religion resides in its basic axioms, the locus of "truth" for that faith. "To live is to suffer," "Jesus is the Christ," "Mohammed is the Messenger of Allah," are "true" respectively for the Buddhist, the Christian, and the Muslim. These assumptions represent the underlying beliefs or standpoint of the man of faith in each religion, and therefore form the background for any systematic summary of each religion.

Since this book is intended for those with little or no firsthand knowledge of the world's religions, its purpose and scope are strictly limited. Our scholarly world is surfeited with facts, and this book is not meant to be an encyclopedia of gods and men. Due to the strictures of space, there also is no opportunity to discuss subtleties of interpretation of theology and philosophy, or to quote extensively from the scriptures. The Western student who is well versed in the literature and history of Judaism and Christianity will find the chapters on these religions sparse and merely suggestive, rather than complete and satisfying. But these more familiar areas have, it is to be hoped, been dealt with in a manner consistent with the approach followed with the less familiar religions of India and East Asia.

Any brief treatment must be selective. What to omit is as important as what to include. Students of anthropology tell us that no society of man has ever been found which did not have some form of religious expression. But it is not possible to include in this brief study all the history of all the societies of man since the dawn of civilization. "The glory that was Greece and the grandeur that was Rome" are part of the heritage of Western culture. Both Greek and Roman civilization had organized religions which, though now defunct, have been studied in great detail in modern times. Yet China and India also had early civilizations that have died out and religions and philosophies that are no longer important. Although the careful student of the history of religions must know a good deal about bygone faiths, classical, Chinese, and Indian, many of which have been rediscovered only in recent decades, we must arbitrarily restrict our survey to the dozen important religions of our day. Only when it is necessary to describe the ancient roots of a living religion will we concern ourselves with the defunct religions.

Another problem is the order in which the religions should be treated. We have chosen simply to move from the more familiar to the less familiar areas of the world. First we present a brief introduction to the nature of religion and to man as a religious being. This section includes a chapter on religion in primitive cultures, for it is assumed that all present-day civilizations have developed out of primitive preliterate societies. We turn then to the four religions of the Bible lands: Judaism, the Persian religion of Zoroaster (which survives today among the Parsis of India), Christianity, and Islam, the faith proclaimed by the prophet Mohammed. From this more familiar area, we then move to the four religions of the Indian subcontinent: Hinduism, the twin heresies of Jainism and Buddhism, and the youngest of the world's religions which we are considering, that of the Sikhs. Finally, we explore East Asia: the Taoist and Confucian religions of China, and the Shinto religion of Japan.

For consistency of approach, and to superimpose some comparative scheme upon these many faiths, we follow the same outline for each religion. This includes, first, a brief description of its land of origin, the people, their language, culture, and historical beginnings, and the basic sacred writings (scriptures) which serve as our primary sources of knowledge. For each religion which has a known founder, we give a brief statement about his life and teachings.

Finally, in order to have a basis for understanding the claim for loyalty which a religion makes upon its followers, we view each in terms of a common scheme. This consists of a sort of systematic theology in which the basic aspects of the religion are considered under seven categories which cover its essential beliefs or world view.

The cosmos. Under this category are included such questions as these: What does the religion teach about the origin and nature of the physical world? What are its conceptions of time and space? Is the world thought to be created, or without beginning or end?

Deity. Since the term *god* has such powerful emotional connotations, the more neutral Latin term is preferred here. Under this heading we ask what view of the supernatural is taught by a religion. Is it panthe-istic, polytheistic, dualistic, and so on? Are its gods actively involved in the affairs of men?

Man. What view of man does this religion hold? Is he thought to be simply an expression of the cosmos? Is he a unique creation? Does he pass through cycles of rebirth and death? What are thought to be his constitutive parts?

Man's plight. In the face of a hostile universe life often appears fraught with peril and even meaningless. What are the kinds of events and situ-ations which threaten man and to what does a given religion attribute the troubles which engulf man and for which he seeks remedies and help? Typical threatening factors are famine, disease, and war, and the fear of death and of demonic powers. Typical causes of man's plight are found in his inherent ignorance, selfishness, or wilful disobedience of a god.

Salvation. With its emphasis upon a creator and savior god whose purpose it is to reward the faithful with a Messianic age, or the bliss of heaven, and to punish the disobedient with the torments of hell, the Judaeo-Christian tradition has tended to cause us to think of "salvation" in terms of one's ultimate destiny. The Latin word *salutas,* however, actually means safety or wholeness and has to do first of all with man's present life, whatever his final destiny may be. Salvation in this sense is the primary concern of all religions. Each religion offers saving help to aid man in warding off trouble and misfortune in this present life; each religion teaches what he must do and believe to achieve a meaningful life secure from fear and want. Conforming to group behavior, sacrificing to gods and ancestors, attempting to live in harmony with the cosmos, or depending upon the help of a saving god—all illustrate the wide va-riety of ways of salvation.

Conduct. It is a truism that all the great religions teach much the same content of ethical living, but it is not so frequently noted that the motivations or sanctions for the good life vary greatly between religions. A primitive man might avoid unsocial behavior for fear of breaking tabus, a Jew or Christian for "fear of the Lord," a Hindu for fear of a lower form of rebirth. In order to indicate the relationship between beliefs and conduct, the ethical sanctions of a religion will be related to the rest of its world view, especially to its teachings about the cosmos, deity, and man.

Destiny. "If a man die shall he live again?" What does the religion teach concerning man's fate after death? How does this teaching relate to the other key concepts of the religion?

The real significance of this outline lies not in the cataloguing of data under each heading, but rather in the interrelation of beliefs within the context of each religion. Thus, a Christian who believes in a creator deity—which implies also belief in a created world, and in man as a being created to obey his God—will consider man's plight, salvation, conduct, and destiny in harmony with these concepts. On the other hand, a Buddhist or Hindu, starting with the conception of man as reborn, will construct doctrines about man's plight, salvation, and destiny which, although consistent in themselves, will differ markedly from those of the Christian, and at strategic points, from one another. Each religion, it is to be hoped, is viewed in its own integrity rather than as simply a collection of ideas and teachings.

Each schematic analysis is followed by a brief summary of the historical development of the religion, its basic sectarian divisions, and its present geographical spread and relative significance. In the case of the three missionary religions, Buddhism, Christianity, and Islam, a fuller treatment is given.

Part One

THE RELIGION OF PRIMITIVE PEOPLES

Chapter One

MAN AND RELIGION

Man is the only known living being who can see himself in perspective, ask about his origins, and contemplate the future of his kind. As man has examined the history of his race he has come to several interesting but humbling conclusions.

MAN AND TIME. Although geophysicists estimate that the earth is approximately four and one-half billion years old and that life has been on this planet for at least one billion years, man as a species has existed for about one million years. In spite of the existence of Homo sapiens for a thousand millenniums, written records go back only about five thousand years. Thus it is obvious that man can never know very much about his beginnings even though, from the point of view of geological time, he is a newcomer to the earth.

MAN AND SPACE. Our sense of the dimensions of human existence has been greatly expanded by the current developments in space travel. Problems that were left in the past to the speculations of the astrophysicist and the philosopher have now become common concern. We have turned from an earth-centered point of view to the question of life on other worlds. In his *Human Destiny* (New York: Longmans, Green & Co., 1947) du Noüy argued that life similar to ours on this planet is mathematically so unlikely to occur by chance alone that it must be labeled a divine miracle. Now, but a couple of decades later, we are told that, in terms of statistical probability, there may be such life as ours on a hundred million planets in the known universe. And the bounds of the known universe are being pushed outward at a fantastic rate as a result of the interpretation of data from such scientific marvels as the electronic telescope.

When we then turn from reflecting upon outer space to considering our own planet, we are confronted with the terrifying facts of the "population explosion." Every day at least a hundred thousand more human beings are born than die. By the year 2000 A.D. the world's population is expected to exceed six billions.

WHAT IS MAN? This age-old question receives fresh attention in every generation. Innumerable attempts have been made to describe man's uniqueness. He is called the only animal who has the ability to laugh at himself, or to make use of fire for warmth and cooking. For our purposes two considerations are important: first, that only man develops societies which create and hand on such tools of civilization as language, traditions of social morality, and the knowledge of pastoral, agrarian, or industrial economy. Second, that man is the only being who appears to practice religion, to attempt to relate himself to powers beyond or outside himself.

WHAT IS SOCIETY? Society is a grouping of persons for mutual protection and help. At least some social organization is necessary with rules and regulations to prevent murder and sexual anarchy, to keep the young from killing off the old and weak, to prevent the strong from seizing and stealing what they choose. Thus virtually all societies have an equivalent of the "Ten Commandments." By such teachings society places the individual under group control, the savage in him is checked, and it becomes gradually possible for men to develop culture and civilization.

WHAT IS RELIGION? Religion usually has to do with man's relationship to the unseen world, to the world of spirits, demons, and gods. A second element common to all religions, and a concept which is central to this guidebook, is the term *salvation.* All religions seek to help man find meaning in a universe which all too often appears to be hostile to his interests. The word *salvation* means, basically, health. It means one is saved *from* disaster, fear, hunger, and a meaningless life. It means one is saved *for* hope, love, security, and the fulfilment of purpose.

In this sense, then, religion is the way in which man seeks meaning in life and hopes to gain help from the unseen or supernatural forces believed to be at work in the universe. This saving help will in turn aid him to avoid evil and to secure positive benefits such as health and long life. Since man is a social being, religion is given concrete expression in the ongoing life of a given society, in myths (stories about the gods in their dealings with the world and its inhabitants), rituals or cultic practices, and, in the case of more advanced civilizations, the creation of sacred writings, or scriptures. It is such expressions of man's religions that we shall describe in the following pages.

THE ORIGINS OF RELIGION. Since the beginning of the modern study of comparative religion by Max Müller about 1875, much has been written on the origins of the world's religions. It is not our concern here to analyze the different approaches that have been taken to this question of origins, especially since this problem cannot be resolved. It is something like the question of the origin of the various languages of the world, or of the so-called races of man. The beginnings of man's religions as well as of the different families of languages, and the origins of the secondary traits of skin color, type of hair, or eye structure, are lost to us simply because they precede our earliest written or oral records.

At the same time it is possible, for our purposes, to sketch as background the conclusions which have received some measure of common acceptance among scholars. It is generally agreed that all religions reach back into prehistoric times. Several theories associated with the names of outstanding pioneers in the study of religious origins indicate both the wide variety of approaches to the problem, and also the general direction in which scholarly opinion has moved. The more important of these theories and the men associated with them follow.

Sir Edward Tylor and the ghost theory. Even before the important pioneering work of Max Müller, a theory of the origin of religion was advanced by Edward Tylor in his study, *Primitive Culture* (1866). Dreams about persons who had died and the belief in ghosts, he held, led to ancestor worship and finally to more developed concepts: important departed ancestors became actual gods.

Max Müller himself stressed an animistic view of religious origins in which he claimed that man personified, or ascribed life and human qualities to such great forces of nature as the sun, the moon, storms, and the sky.

Sir James G. Frazer. The famous author of the exhaustive study, *The Golden Bough,* found the origins of religion in attempts by primitive man to control the world of nature, and the unseen world as well, by magic. Magic he defined as an organized attempt to coerce nature's forces to do man's bidding.

Andrew Lang and Father Wilhelm Schmidt. The Scotsman, Lang, and later the Austrian, Schmidt, championed, by excellent research, the orthodox biblical notion that all mankind at one time practiced a primitive monotheism.

Professor Codrington and the concept of mana. In 1891 Bishop Codrington published *The Melanesians,* in which he introduced the concept of *mana.* Mana is a term widely used in the Islands of the South Pacific to refer to the supernatural power which is believed to reside in all things and to motivate all life and activity. Since this concept appears to characterize the world view of most primitive peoples, the anthropologist, R. R. Marett, and other students of religion have employed the term mana in a technical sense to refer to this phenomenon.

Sigmund Freud and Carl Jung. Perhaps it is misleading to link these two psychoanalysts, but the teacher and his often dissident student held a somewhat similar view of religion. Freud's position on religion was the culmination of the work of a long series of scholars who had claimed that religion is a projection of one's fears and loyalties. Freud's contribution lies in his claim that religion is the expression of neuroses, based on the guilt inherent in repression of infantile sexual fantasies. Jung traced the archetypes of our individual thoughts and actions to the unconscious racial history of man, and suggested that religion represents the method mankind has developed to live with those fears and frustrations which have been built into our subconscious. Of late, students of Indian thought have used Jung's theories of a racial unconscious to illustrate and defend the Hindu belief in rebirth.

Rudolf Otto. In his *The Idea of the Holy* this German theologian applied such concepts as that of mana to the realm of theology and found that man's religious experiences tend to prove the existence of an unseen force, the *numinous,* before which man stands in awe, and with which he has real interaction.

CURRENT DEVELOPMENTS IN HISTORY OF RELIGIONS. In recent decades such scholars as G. van der Leeuw, Joachim Wach, and Mircea Eliade have stressed the sociological and phenomenological study of religion. In their attempts to establish a scientific basis for the study of religions, they use a descriptive approach, which makes it necessary to consider seriously all experience of religious phenomena, physical or supernatural.

This brief summary of a century of development in the study of religious origins should indicate that the problem is important, but insolvable. In our approach, we draw upon the available materials to describe, rather than to explain, man's religions; to facilitate our description, the world's religions are classified into four groups and each group is treated as a larger unit. These four classes are (1) the religious outlook of primitive or preliterate peoples; (2) the outlook of world view represented by the monotheistic religions of biblical lands; (3) the world view represented by the religions of India, and (4) that represented by the nature and ancestor worship of the religions of China and Japan.

A WORKING CLASSIFICATION OF RELIGIONS. Although there is much overlapping between some religions, and although an increasing number of persons, especially in western Europe, North America, and the countries now under Communist influence, deny any religious affiliation, the approximately three billion people in the world may be divided according to religious classification as follows:

Primitive peoples. Uncivilized, preliterate, scattered around the world, but concentrated in Central Africa, South America, North Asia and the Pacific Islands, these number about two hundred millions. The religious point of view common to such peoples underlies that of the three other groups of religions.

Members of religions originating in biblical lands. Judaism, Zoroastrianism (Parsis), Christianity, and Islam claim approximately one and one-quarter billion people. These religions hold in common several basic beliefs, separating them from the other three groups. These are belief in a single, creator god (monotheism), in a real world of time and space in which each person is placed (created) for a single life span, and in a destiny of reward or punishment based upon one's belief and practice in this earthly life.

Members of religions originating in India. Hinduism, Jainism, Buddhism, Sikhism claim about six hundred million people in South Asia. In common these hold that each person is reborn into this present world according to the deeds (*karma*) of a previous life, and that man's highest destiny is to escape this cycle of rebirth.

Members of religions of East Asia. Taoism, Confucianism, and Shintoism claim about one billion believers under their influence. They are blended with various forms of Buddhism. Although they maintain the importance of this present world of time and space, these religions have no creator god in the biblical sense. Instead, the two elements of nature and ancestor worship are blended with varying emphasis and degree.

Chapter Two

THE RELIGION OF PRIMITIVE PEOPLES

A primitive society may be characterized as one which has not developed a written language. The many careful studies which have been made of such preliterate societies lead to the conclusion that the world view and religious practices of such societies have much in common. For this reason it is customary to abstract the common elements and to generalize about primitive religion on the basis of such an abstract analysis.

THE NATURE OF PRIMITIVE SOCIETY. There are no physical or mental differences between primitive and civilized man, but primitive society exists at a simple level. Food is obtained by fishing and hunting, and there is minimum knowledge and use of agriculture. The society is characterized by group behavior and little or no social stratification. There is no leisured, rich class, and also no slave class which would permit the luxury of the development of such skills as writing. (Since every civilization grew out of a primitive and preliterate society, and often the oral traditions of the primitive group were committed to writing at the later, civilized stage, some continuity between primitive and more advanced societies exists.) The cultural level and economic organization of various primitive societies may differ, but in each case, its knowledge of the rest of the world is limited and the society is static rather than dynamic.

THE LOCATION OF PRIMITIVE PEOPLES. Since one distinctive trait of a primitive society is its preliteracy, it is not surprising that such societies are mostly to be found in out-of-the-way corners of the world. Such backwaters consist of the following:

Backwaters of time. Although there is no way of proving that prehistoric man held religious views similar to those of contemporary primitives, all evidence points to this. Archaeological findings of early altars, figures of idols, and surviving traditions in later written records lead to what would appear to be a commonsense conclusion—that the religion of early man was the typical magic and superstition of today's primitives.

Geographical backwaters. Such out-of-the-way places as Central Africa, northern Siberia, the basin of the Amazon River, the jungles of India and Borneo contain tens of millions who have had little contact with civilization, either Asian or Western. These groups have been a happy hunting ground for anthropologists who have assembled a mass of valuable data about primitive societies which aids our analysis of the nature of primitive religion.

Religious backwaters. Although the major religions have their roots in prehistoric times, their known development generally begins somewhat later. But not only do primitive traits survive; much more important is the fact that the primitive nature in each of us all too often finds expression within the context of a so-called higher religion. We talk glibly about the practice of magic and the worship of idols among African tribes, but we often overlook such low or uncivilized practices among Christians as snake handling, the outrages of the Ku Klux Klan, or the omission of a thirteenth floor in skyscrapers.

Not only do we practice "primitive religion" in group behavior, but the same type of superstition exists in most individuals. The use of a lucky rabbit's foot and throwing salt over one's shoulder are common illustrations. But interest in astrology and the millions spent on it every year also attests to the primitive level of much of our thinking. In fact, it is too easy to criticize such beliefs and practices; we seek to understand and evaluate them in positive terms too seldom.

THE CHARACTERISTICS OF PRIMITIVE RELIGION. Often primitive religion is called such disparaging names as "magic," "superstition," "early," "prescientific." All of these sophisticated labels may fit, but do not help us to understand the values and functions of the religions. It is perhaps just as sound to label all sensual enjoyment, such as eating and drinking, a normal married sex life, playing games, or even sleeping as "gluttony," "licentiousness," "frivolity," or "laziness." One of the probable results of the development of education and the stress upon reason and science is that any emotional approach to life is quickly criticized. Yet modern Germany, with the finest universities, a high development of the natural sciences, and the reputation for being a great center of reason and naturalism also became the home of Nazi practices of a most barbaric nature. We all live much more by emotions than we wish to admit; this makes it possible for us to have some appreciation of the nature and values of primitive religion.

THE PRIMITIVE WORLD. Emotional awareness and response

to the world is basic to the world view of the primitive. We think of the small child who is afraid of the dark, or who kicks at a chair as though it could be punished for getting in his way. But the adult is also apt to kick at a chair over which he has stumbled in the dark, and to blame his automobile when it breaks down. We talk about heart attacks and seizures, strokes and lunacy—all terms which originate in a primitive or prescientific awareness of the world.

To the primitive, a fire which threatens the village is alive. He does not set a backfire or seek to beat out the fire with branches. Instead, he flees from the fire before it "gets him," or perhaps the village organizes a group to frighten away the fire with shouting and the banging of kettles. Disease stalks the village and must be frightened, cajoled, or driven away, often with nauseous stenches. The whole world is full of power which can help or hurt, and man must be alert to danger and opportunity. This basic notion of aliveness in the world and the various methods used to control and coerce phenomena are expressed by anthropologists in terms taken from primitive societies.

Mana. As we have said earlier, this word has been used since Bishop Codrington's pioneer work to express the primitive concept of power immanent in the world. Although many anthropologists question the presence of mana in all primitive cultures, for our purposes it helps to describe the nature of the primitive's awareness of his world. Mana represents the force which enters into things to cause them to act. The sun burns the skin or causes vapor to rise on water because of the strength of mana. If a stream floods its banks and wipes out a village, mana caused it to do so. If a limb falls from a tree and narrowly misses a hunter, the limb is motivated by mana. Electricity does much in reality that the primitive ascribes to mana. Electricity's power can cause a fire, shock one to death, light the house and cook one's breakfast. If it is properly channeled, all is well. If not contained, this naked force can do harm rather than good. Yet electricity is neither good nor bad. Like mana, it is simply energy in action.

Tabu. This Polynesian term (actually, *tapu*) is used to describe one of the ways of controlling mana and preventing evil effects. An action or an object which is tabu must be avoided since the deed or object could unleash mana harmful to the individual or his tribe. Tabu channels mana, protecting the villagers from possible evil. Since mana is unpredictable or capricious, certain safeguards must constantly be exercised by society. Although sometimes the connection made by primitives between an event and good or evil results is consistent and meaningful, more often it is an arbitrary "playing safe." The Latin phrase, *post hoc, ergo propter hoc,* which might be paraphrased, "happening after this, therefore caused by this," is often used to express this lack of analyzed cause and effect. If twins are born in a village the night a terrible storm strikes, twins become dangerous, i.e., tabu. Ten miles away twins might be considered good luck because of a different coincidence. If a man dies while drinking from a spring, it may be thought that the spring killed him. The spring might be labeled tabu to protect the other villagers.

Fetish. From the Portuguese *feitiço,* "made" or "created," this refers to a sort of charm used by its owner to channel mana for his good, and to ward off evil. The rabbit's foot, the lucky coin, or similar devices are benign examples. The West African fetish is usually more elaborate, but its purpose is identical.

Animism. Although some scholars continue to follow Tylor and Max Müller in referring to primitive religion as animism, this term would appear to represent an advance over the more simple concept of mana. The Latin term *anima* means soul, and animism refers to the primitive practice of ascribing souls or individuality, not only to men and animals, but to the world of things as well. Thus any object like a stone, tree, mountain, or stream, or phenomenon of nature, such as sunlight, wind, or rain, might possess individuality. This would appear to be mana in a more localized form and therefore also subject to control by tabus and fetishes. It is assumed that animism can lead to the worship of sacred mountains or trees, and of the forces of nature.

Magic. This term is used to describe primitive attempts to control the unseen world of mana, such as traditional dances to cause game to appear, or to cause rain by imitating it in motion. Magic is primarily an attempt to coerce the unseen forces of nature to do man's bidding.

The medicine man. One who has this role is very important in a primitive society. He has learned the secrets of mana and has the knowledge and skills to control and channel mana for good, and to avoid its harmful effects. His leadership is accepted for the same reason that tabus are followed. Since tabus are believed to have worked in the past, no one is willing to risk disaster by attempting something new.

THE PRIMITIVE'S WORLD VIEW. Using the definitions above, let us set down a systematic statement of primitive religion according to the scheme described in the Introduction.

The cosmos. The world of primitive man has limited horizons. The primitive lives in a world that is alive, but he has little knowledge of what lies on the other side of the mountain or river. His society may possess some simple myths about a first man or the creation of the world, but this is not usual. Time, for him, is also a vague concept; such divisions of time as weeks, months, and years may be unknown; even seasons as designations of time might pass unnoticed.

Deity. Conceptions of the supernatural world vary in different primitive societies. Polytheism, polydaemonism, ancestor worship, nature worship, a single sky or sun god, and combinations of these and other concepts are to be found. All attempts to show a common origin for such beliefs, or to show that each is at some stage progressing toward a "high god" have been unsuccessful. But a common denominator for all primitive conceptions of divinity has been found in the sense of living power in the world described above under the term mana. If ancestors are worshiped, or at least respected, it is assumed to be because they retain some mana which can be used for good or evil; therefore ancestors are placated with food and other gifts. If the thunderstorm is treated with respect and personified, it is in order that its capricious mana may better be controlled. It would appear that mana is easier to live with if it is localized and labeled.

Man. Primitive man's concept of his own nature is as limited as his view of the universe. The two distinctive elements of a primitive anthropology are (1) that man is akin to the world of animals, and even to the inanimate, and (2) that man is first of all a member of a group. Man can be brother to the wolf or bear; the force which causes plants to grow and rivers to flow also activates man. And the real distinction between human beings and other beings is that man is a member of a human society.

Man's plight. Assuming that all religion begins with man's need for help in his struggle to maintain life and to find meaning in it, we see that for the primitive there are two basic sources of trouble. First, the capricious potency of mana must be channeled correctly. Sickness, failure to find or kill game, flood, storm, fire, defeat by the enemy, all are caused by dangerous mana. Each society works out a way of living with this dangerous power, and all must abide by the rules agreed upon by custom. Therefore to break a tabu, either deliberately or unintentionally, causes trouble. Disease is not blamed upon poor sanitation or contagion, in our sense of these terms. It is assumed that mana is at work for evil because a tabu has been broken, or because of some error in the carefully guided behavior of the individual or the tribe.

The corollary to this is that it is dangerous to act and to think as an individual. Man is a member of the group and must think and act in the same way as everyone else. If he does not, he is like an individual standing up in a canoe full of people and doing acrobatic stunts; he might easily upset the canoe and all might perish. Thus individualistic behavior is often tabu and even almost unthinkable.

Salvation. In order to be saved from disasters and to achieve the good things of life, the primitive must observe tabus and be as much as possible a good and cooperating member of his society. At the same time, the group places itself under the control of the medicine man, who has superior knowledge of the capricious ways of mana and has the ability to cope with this dangerous force. If all tabus are rigorously observed, if all members of the society work as a single unit and follow the teachings of the witch doctor, it is to be hoped that illness will be avoided, food will be plentiful, the enemy will be defeated, and evil beasts and demons will lose their power to harm. For the individual, possession of a fetish will be efficacious in channeling mana for good rather than evil.

Conduct. It has been pointed out above that a certain minimum of ethical practice is necessary for any society to exist. There must be laws forbidding or regulating murder, incest, stealing, and bearing false witness or else anarchy takes over. What motivates the primitive man to observe the rules of good conduct in his society? This motivation is closely linked with the requirements for salvation in this present life. To murder is tabu, for it might bring evil mana upon the murderer or the group. If marriage outside the tribe is tabu, the tribe practices endogamy; if marriage within the tribe is tabu, exogamy. The motivation and content of ethical conduct is determined by conformity to the group and this, in turn, by what has become accepted as the best way to control mana.

Destiny. What happens at death? If mana causes man to breathe and to remain warm and alive, death must be the loss of mana. But if one can dream of a person who is known to be miles away, or who has been dead for some time, perhaps this individual mana can survive death or leave one's body for a time. Though many primitive societies have no clear teaching about life after death, a common notion is that some continuation of the force of the individual mana is possible. Great heroes who have an extra amount of mana, evil witch doctors who terrorize their tribes, and others with unusual endowments may survive longer in death than those with less mana. Since these departed ancestors would remain around the village after death, the graveyard is a locale tabu where such ancestors rove and are a possible threat, especially if they are vengeful. Gifts of food and other useful objects are left for the spirits, to placate them and to solicit their help in time of crisis. Destiny, therefore, for the primitive, may be to survive death as a shade and to last long or to fade soon, depending on the amount of mana one had possessed in life.

AN EVALUATION OF PRIMITIVISM. Societies existing at the level of mere subsistence are threatened on every hand. Starvation and disease may wipe out the tribe without warning. Since the world is full of terror, any means to make it possible to live with this terror is of value. The individual finds a sense of security and well-being by following the dicta of the tribe and being a good member of society. The society in turn stays on an even keel by means of such group conformity. Instead of constant fear, there is group solidarity and its attendant values.

On the other hand, since the emphasis is upon survival, any new action or idea is opposed as dangerous. The old is passed on from generation to generation, and the emphasis upon physical survival carries over to the area of ideas. Power is concentrated in the hands of the medicine man who might be neurotic, vengeful, and debauched. New leadership has difficulty in establishing itself, the false is propagated without challenge, and the society, caught in a vicious circle, can raise itself above the primitive level only with great difficulty.

In the succeeding chapters the leading living religions, each of which arose out of a primitive background, or branched out from a religion whose origins were primitive, are discussed. But the "primitive" can also be called *primary,* and no religion completely transcends its origins, nor should it attempt to do so. As a primitive society rises above the level of mere subsistence and develops a leisure class, cultivates the art of writing, and produces a literature, the intellectual approach to religion comes to the fore. But the emotional awareness of the sacred or holy, which characterizes primitive religion, underlies all the religions of mankind. This fact is presupposed in the rest of this book, although the emphasis is upon religion as reflected in scriptures and theology.

Part Two

THE RELIGIONS OF
BIBLICAL LANDS

Chapter Three

THE ANCIENT NEAR EAST

The semiarid land known as the Near East, which includes Palestine, the Arabian Peninsula, and Iran, has seen the rise of four of the world's living religions. These religions—Judaism, Zoroastrianism, Christianity, and Islam—have certain basic characteristics in common. Because of the proximity of their origins, the influences that they have exchanged, and their common characteristics, they are treated as a group. This chapter presents a general introduction to the common background of these "biblical" religions. A broad treatment of the more important geographical, historical, and cultural factors will aid our analysis of the structure and message of each of these religions.

THE CRADLE OF CIVILIZATION. J. H. Breasted gave the name "the Fertile Crescent" to the sweep of land that stretches from the Persian Gulf on the east, northwestward through Mesopotamia, and which swings southeast through Palestine into the Nile Valley. This area has also been called the "cradle of civilization," since two of the earliest centers of civilization were in the Nile Valley of Egypt and the Mesopotamian valley of the Tigris and Euphrates rivers. The cultures and religions which arose in these two favored areas have long since disappeared. Their influence has survived, however, for Egyptian, Babylonian, and Assyrian religion strongly influenced not only the thought of the Greeks and Romans, but also more directly the ethics and theology of the Hebrews.

On the other hand, it was out of the semiarid area of Palestine, the harsh deserts of Arabia, and the semiarid plateau of Iran that living religions emerged. Just as the fertile valleys of the Nile and of Mesopotamia helped to make early development of writing, architecture, and surveying possible, the harshness of life in the adjacent regions probably helps to explain the rise of these four monotheistic religions. Thus, for instance, Palestine is cruelly located in a narrow belt of land between the sea on the west and the desert on the east. Sustaining life is not easy in this area. The narrow land also serves as a corridor across which armies have marched from earliest times. Palestine was a buffer between Egypt on the one hand and the imperialistic designs of the Babylonians, Hittites, and Assyrians on the other. Later the Persians, Greeks, and Romans ruled Palestine using the area both as a corridor and as a buffer against their enemies. Similarly, life in the Iran of Zoroaster or the Arabia of Mohammed was characterized more by struggle than by leisure.

This intense involvement, both with the land in the struggle for economic survival, and with the constant warfare and international intrigue which afflicted these areas, partially accounts for the emphasis each of these religions gives to the concept of a creator god. These religions also all view history as the arena wherein man must struggle and make ethical choices, and in which a creator god reveals his purpose for man's salvation. As we shall see, this is in radical contrast to the view of god and history which characterizes the religions of India and China, both of which developed in "river valley" cultures.

THE PEOPLES OF BIBLICAL LANDS. Because so many peoples and cultures shared this area, it is not possible to discuss them all. Some general comments, however, are in order. In the Fertile Crescent and Arabia, the dominant ethnic (linguistic) group was *Semitic.* This term, taken from the name of one of the sons of Noah, Shem, refers primarily to a family of languages. The Hebrews, Phoenicians, Babylonians, Assyrians, and to some extent the Egyptians, employed Semitic speech. Into this area at times came invaders who used some form of the Indo-European family of languages—the Hittites, Persians, Greeks, and Romans. (The scriptures of Zoroastrianism are in Persian, an Indo-European language.)

The order in which we shall survey this group of religions is based partly on chronology and partly on logic. The earliest of the living religions which arose in the Near East is Judaism. This religion will be described, first in its classical expression, and then in the form in which it survived the rise of Christianity, and has developed down to modern times. Next, the religion of Zoroaster will be summarized. This movement began in Persia, probably in the sixth century B.C., and strongly influenced both Judaism and Christianity, which in turn became one of the three missionary religions of the world. Last, the other missionary religion to come out of this area, Islam, the religion founded by Mohammed, will be considered.

COMMON ELEMENTS IN THE MONOTHEISTIC RELIGIONS. The religions of the world can be divided into three basic groupings—that of the Near East, just referred to, those of India, and those of East Asia. At least three presuppositions or basic teachings, which are held more or less in common by the four religions of biblical lands, set them off from the religions of the other two areas. These common elements are:

A creator god. Although the name or designation for the god of each of these religions is different, in each case he is conceived as creator of the world and the final judge and savior of the men he has created. He also is proclaimed as the only true god, and the worship of any other god is condemned as apostasy.

Man. In each of these religions man is held to be a creature, created by his god, whose duty it is to obey that god. Man has but one life to live in this world of time and space. A vital aspect of his nature is that he is endowed with the freedom to choose to serve the true god, or to be disloyal by serving a "false" god.

History as revelation. Each of these monotheistic religions places emphasis on the power and purpose of a creator god. One way in which this finds expression is in the concern for eschatology, in the importance given to myths about the future purpose of the god for his creation. Just as the god created an idyllic garden of Eden for the blissful existence of the first human couple before disobedience brought pain, sorrow, and death, so too will this god someday redeem his creation. For these religions, then, history is a creation of god; in it evil is recognized as a fact of existence. But it is believed that god someday will destroy all opposition to his will, bringing an end to history, and establishing his kingdom or rule. Accordingly, one of the characteristics of these religions is a concern for the final destiny of each individual and of the world, since the final judgment resides in the hands of god.

Whatever the ultimate destiny of the individual and the race, man needs to know and follow the will of the god in this present life. Each of these religions proclaims a god who has revealed his will to man in the events of history, and through his human spokesmen called *prophets*. The various disclosures of god's purpose for man are preserved in the scriptures of the religion. Although the religions of India and East Asia also have prophets and sacred writings, there is a greater emphasis in the biblical religions upon the scriptures as containing final, revealed truth, essential to salvation. It is not knowledge of revealed truth, but the necessity of the faithful to obey the revealed will of the god that characterizes the prophetic, monotheistic religions.

Chapter Four

JUDAISM

Since Judaism is intimately linked with its Holy Land, Palestine, any understanding of this religion should begin with the history of that land and its peoples. Palestine was one of the important crossroads of classical times, serving as the arena for a constant interplay of cultures; this exposed the inhabitants to a wide range of religious ideas, values, and cultic practices. The Egyptians, Phoenicians, Babylonians, Assyrians, Persians, Greeks, and Romans all influenced the physical and spiritual lives of the Jews. Thus, in the history of Judaism in biblical times there is apparent a definite expansion of theological statement and understanding. Yet certain early premises and convictions of the Hebrews remain constant to this day. In the following summary of Judaism, the classical Hebrew religion will first be outlined, and subsequent refinements and ramifications will be described in relation to this early religious outlook.

THE INHABITANTS OF PALESTINE. In the previous chapter, we have mentioned the peoples of the Fertile Crescent. In Palestine itself two important groups require comment: the Canaanites, a Semitic-speaking people closely related to the Phoenicians, who also were of the same stock as the Hebrews who invaded their land about 1100 B.C.; and the Philistines, who gave their name to the land of Palestine. The latter were from southern Greece, or possibly Crete, and were driven out by northern invaders in the twelfth century B.C. After trying in vain to land on the coast of Egypt, some of them invaded the southwest coast of Palestine. Here they established a group of city-states, somewhat on the Greek plan. They brought with them knowledge of iron-smelting and accordingly exercised a military influence out of proportion to their numerical strength. During the Hebrew conquest of Palestine, the invaders had to come to terms with both the Canaanites and the Philistines before they could establish a stable kingdom.

THE HEBREWS. The term *Hebrew* is thought by many scholars to derive from the word *'Ibri,* which appears around 1500 B.C. in the tablets from Tell el-Amarna in Egypt, or from the word *Hapiru* occurring in the Nuzu tablets from Mesopotamia. The term *'Ibri* probably means "to cross over" and may refer to desert border raiders living on the fringes of the Fertile Crescent. If so, the designation *Hebrew* would be a general term applying to various groups of warlike, semicivilized tribes of nomads living in the desert bordering Palestine. In later centuries, this term came to be restricted to those Hebrews who became, after 1050 B.C., the rulers of Palestine under the Hebrew kings, Saul and his successors.

ISRAELITES AND JEWS. After the establishment of the Hebrew kingdom in Palestine, this group of Semitic peoples also referred to themselves as *Israelites,* because of a legend that the twelve tribes of Hebrews united under Saul and David were descended from a common ancestor, Jacob, also called *Israel.* His twelve sons were the ancestors of the twelve tribes of Israel. After 721 B.C., only the tribe of Judah survived the ravages of the Assyrians. From this tribal name came the terms *Judean* and *Jew.* In modern times, the German adjective *jüdisch* gave rise to the word *Yiddish.* It is the traditions and religion of the Israelites that we now trace as the beginning of the story of Judaism.

EARLY HEBREW RELIGION (1250-539 B.C.)

SOURCES FOR CLASSICAL HEBREW RELIGION. For the recovery of Hebrew religion up to the end of the Babylonian Exile, our primary source is the early portion of the Hebrew Bible (the Christian Old Testament). Although a clearcut chronological division is not possible, the first two divisions of the threefold scriptures, "The Law, the Prophets, and the Writings," are mostly pre-exilic or from the time of the Exile.

The Law. The Hebrew term for the first portion of Jewish scripture is *Torah,* which means "law" or "teaching," and by usage has come to be a general word for divine revelation. The Torah consists of the first five books of the Old Testament, containing myth, legend, history, and religious law. Its present form was shaped about 450 B.C. during the Persian rule of Palestine. Tradition ascribes it to Moses (about 1200 B.C.), but it is now considered a composite document representing at least five hundred years of growth, both in oral and written form; its final compilation was achieved after the Exile.

The Prophets. This second division of scripture was completed about

200 B.C., and contains both books of history written from the prophetic point of view and books containing the actual sermons and teachings of the Hebrew prophets.

Other sources. Owing to the intense activity of generations of Jewish and Christian scholars in the field of Old Testament studies, a wealth of pertinent writings from Egypt and the Fertile Crescent during this period has been discovered, translated, and interpreted; this makes possible an understanding of the early Hebrew scriptures far beyond all other sacred writings except the New Testament.

MOSES AND THE BEGINNINGS OF HEBREW RELIGION. Although Judaism is the religion of a people who trace their origins back to Abraham (1750 B.C.), the real beginnings probably are to be linked with Moses, "the Lawgiver." About 1300 B.C., some of the Israelite Hebrews were in Egypt serving as slaves to the Egyptians. To them came Moses with a twofold message: a god who revealed his name to be Yahweh (Jehovah) had appeared to him in the desert of Midian, directing him to go to Egypt and lead the Israelites out of bondage. Moses reported to the Israelites that Yahweh had chosen them to be his particular people and had promised to save them by his power.

THE EXODUS. This promise of Yahweh to save his people was dramatically fulfilled when the Israelites fled from Egypt. The Egyptians pursued them and caught up with them at the Red Sea (the Hebrew text reads Sea of Reeds). One early account tells how an east wind blew all night, drying up the shallow waters of the Sea of Reeds. The Israelites walked across a crust of dried mud to safety, but when the Egyptians pursued with their horses and chariots, the chariot wheels became clogged in the mud and the Egyptians turned back. This event proved to the Israelites the truth of Yahweh's power to save them, and at Mount Sinai, under Moses' leadership, they entered into a covenant with Yahweh. The subsequent history of the Israelites is interpreted in terms of their understanding of the purpose which their god, Yahweh, has for them in this covenantal relationship.

HISTORY AND REVELATION. Although the Exodus continued to be regarded as the event above all which proved Yahweh's power to save and guide his chosen people, the problem of the content of Yahweh's will for his people remained. In one sense, the real story of Judaism is the story of the various ways in which its religious leaders gave expression to their understanding of what Yahweh required of his people. Thus, the priests stressed the Law, claiming that the covenant between Yahweh and the Israelites must find expression in certain cultic demands. Although the Law of the priests included a demand for social morality, sacrifice and observance of ritualistic forms were emphasized. The prophets, who claimed to be spokesmen for Yahweh, stressed ethical obedience above sacrifice and ritual. The classic prophetic statement is in Micah 6:6-8:

With what shall I come before Yahweh, and bow myself before God on high?

Shall I come before him with burnt offerings, with calves a year old?

Will Yahweh be pleased with thousands of rams, with ten thousands of rivers of oil?

Shall I give my first-born for my transgression, the fruit of my body for the sin of my soul?

He has showed you, O man, what is good; and what does Yahweh require of you

But to do justice, and to love kindness, and to walk humbly with your God? *

Not only had Yahweh made a covenant with his people through revelation; the people also were held responsible for their actions and warned that any failure to fulfill their part of the covenant would be punished, just as obedience would be blessed. This is a new concept in the history of religion. Although, for example, the religion of the Canaanites taught that the god Baal would aid his worshipers if they asked for his help, we search in vain for mention of ethical or moral demands upon the Canaanites by their deity. Yahweh, on the other hand, was concerned with morality, and the entire history of the Israelites centers on the notion of responsibility and the conviction that obedience would bring blessing, but disobedience would lead to adversity.

PRE-EXILIC JUDAISM'S WORLD VIEW. Let us now apply our seven-point scheme to classic Hebrew religion in order to summarize its essential teachings and to indicate the basis for the new direction which was taken by post-exilic Judaism.

---

* Quotations are from the *Revised Standard Version of the Holy Bible,* copyright 1946 and 1952 by the Division of Christian Education of the National Council of the Churches of Christ in the United States of America, and are used by permission.

The cosmos. The world was created by Yahweh at the beginning of time. The early mythology of the Hebrews (Genesis 1-11) projects their faith back into prehistory, telling how Yahweh created the heavens and the earth. The cosmos consisted of three levels: the heavens, the earth, and an underworld, called *Sheol.*

Deity. Although many gods might exist and be served by various people, for the true believer there is but one god, Yahweh, who is to be worshiped and obeyed to the exclusion of all other gods. Yahweh has three basic characteristics: he is creator of the world and its inhabitants; he has the power to control his creation and therefore to come to the aid of his chosen people when he pleases; and finally, he has a purpose for his creation which he will fulfill even if it means the destruction of those who oppose or flaunt his will. Thus Yahweh is creator, savior, and judge.

Man. Man is placed in the world by Yahweh, and man's duty is to obey his creator. In an early myth in Genesis (Genesis 2:4b-3:24, c. 850 B.C.), Yahweh forms man from the dust of the earth and breathes life into him. Man is thus akin to the animals, but unlike them he is commanded to obey Yahweh and also has freedom to choose. He can choose to serve Yahweh, or to disobey. Man has but one life in which to be rewarded or punished.

Man's plight. Yahweh made a covenant with his people, Israel, and as creator and lord of history, he controls all that happens. Therefore, such evils as defeat in battle, famine, disease, or barrenness in women were ascribed to failure to fulfill Yahweh's will. The cause of man's troubles was the sin of disobedience. Basically, this occurs in two forms: following one's own selfish interests rather than the revealed will of Yahweh and—a more serious offense—serving some god other than Yahweh. One might choose to serve the Canaanite god, Baal, or the goddess Ishtar of the Babylonians, for instance, but one must expect to suffer for apostasy. Part of the ancient confession of Israel, the *Shema,* states:

You shall fear Yahweh your God; you shall serve him, and swear by his name. You shall not go after other gods, of the gods of the peoples who are round about you; for Yahweh your God in the midst of you is a jealous God: lest the anger of the Yahweh your God be kindled against you, and he destroy you from off the face of the earth. (Deut. 6:13-15; 650 B.C.)

Salvation. In the pre-exilic period, salvation was closely linked to obedience. If Yahweh were served to the exclusion of all other loyalties and if his will were followed, as taught by the religious leaders, peace, prosperity, and happiness would follow, as day follows night. Since peace and prosperity, health and happiness were not always present in full measure, at first it was easy to discover the cause of trouble. The prophets blamed disaster upon apostasy and moral degradation, and called for a return to Yahweh and his righteousness. The priests, for their part, clamored for more sacrifices and closer attention to ritual. Both emphasized group salvation, and the welfare of the individual was identified with that of the nation. Nevertheless, although the nation was called upon to fulfill its part of the covenant with Yahweh, Israel's god was regarded as the true source of salvation, possessing the power to save and to destroy, to reward and to punish.

Conduct. Because salvation was based upon obedience to the will of Yahweh, and because the prophetic stress was upon social morality as part of Yahweh's requirements, the ethical content of pre-exilic Judaism was unequaled in early times, especially in the area of social concern. The sanction, or motivation for ethical living, again involved obedience to Yahweh. Both the desire to please Yahweh by fulfilling his covenant demands, and the fear of his punishment, were advanced as reasons for ethical living.

Destiny. Early Judaism has no clear teaching on individual destiny. The usual primitive notion of temporary survival in the form of a shade or spirit is found. Only the very great would survive, and even these but for a time, as ancestors in an underground abode known as *Sheol.* A social destiny was reflected in the belief that Yahweh had ordained a future day when he would restore the fortunes of his people. But even this social destiny was regarded, at least by prophets such as Amos (750 B.C.), as a day of punishment and doom, rather than fulfilment, because of the nation's sins. (Cf. Amos 5:18-20.)

THE RISE AND DEVELOPMENT OF RABBINIC JUDAISM
(500 B.C.-500 A.D.)

The destruction of Jerusalem and of the Temple of Solomon by the Babylonians in 587 B.C. and the deportation of the flower of the nation to Babylon was a blow that would have meant the end of most nations and religions. But in exile Judaism survived both as a nation and as a religion, interpreting the debacle of the Exile as a just punishment for the sins and apostasy of the people. From this time, the name *Judaism* is used to designate the main movement of the religion which developed out of the pattern of survival formulated during the experience of the Exile.

The Persians under Cyrus conquered Babylon in 539, and within a year or two after this date, Cyrus published an edict permitting the Jews to return to their homeland. The return of the former captives was slow and went on for several centuries (until 165 B.C.). During this period, they continued under Persian and Greek rule. Jerusalem was rebuilt; the Temple was reconstructed, and Judaism as a religion became strong again. Then, after a century of independence under the Maccabees (165-63 B.C.), the Romans occupied Palestine. Although at first the Romans allowed the Jews a measure of local rule under the Herods, a bloody insurrection (66-70 A.D.) led to the sack of Jerusalem and the destruction of Herod's Temple. A final revolt (132-135 A.D.), under Bar Kochbah, resulted in the loss of Palestine as a Jewish homeland until the establishment of the state of Israel in 1948. Out of this tangled history emerged both the Jewish sect, Christianity, and Rabbinic Judaism, which became the main stream of Judaism in the West.

SOURCES FOR RABBINIC JUDAISM. The formative period for Rabbinic Judaism extends from the end of the Babylonian Exile to the completion of the Talmud, or the thousand years from about 500 B.C. to 500 A.D. Among the wealth of literary sources for this millennium, the following are significant.

The Hebrew Bible. Although the early portions of the Old Testament have been cited as sources for pre-exilic Judaism, the Jewish scriptures took their final form only after the Exile, when many of them were written. The Book of Leviticus in the Torah; postexilic prophetic writings, such as Haggai, Zechariah, and Joel; and, in their final form, the division of Jewish scriptures known as the *Writings* (including Daniel) come from the postexilic period. The Hebrew Bible was completed by 90 A.D., when the Council at Jamnia agreed upon the contents in their present form.

The Apocrypha. After the conquests of Alexander the Great (died 323 B.C.), the Hebrew scriptures began to be translated into Greek for Jews living outside of Palestine. Some fourteen books or writings were then added to the existing scriptures. All of these—which are included in the Christian Bible as the Apocrypha—were written during the centuries immediately before and after the beginning of the Christian era and tell us much about Jewish religious thought of that time.

The Pseudepigrapha. This is a collection of extra-canonical Jewish writings from this period which biblical scholars have made during the last hundred years. It is a primary source for the various sectarian movements in Judaism. The most recent addition to this collection is the famous Dead Sea Scrolls.

Others. Several key sources inform us about the first century A.D. The writings of the Alexandrian Jew, *Philo Judaeus* (c. 20 B.C.-50 A.D.), relate Jewish religious thought to Greek philosophy; *Flavius Josephus* (37-95 A.D.) wrote a detailed Jewish history of this period; and the Christian New Testament relates the rise of the Jewish sect which developed into Christianity.

The Mishnah. After 450 B.C., when the Torah as a written document was completed, each generation produced scholars who sought to make the Law relevant for their time. Their teachings were preserved in oral form and became so extensive that memorization became difficult. About 200 A.D. the oral tradition was codified into six tractates and written down as the Mishnah, or the Repetition. This runs to a thousand pages in English and consists primarily of directions for daily living known as *Halakah,* or "the way to walk" (i.e., live). This is the real basis of Rabbinic teaching.

The Talmud. About 500 A.D. another recension of Jewish learning was compiled, based upon the Mishnah but containing much more material, especially didactic stories known as *Haggadah.* In English, this runs to thirty-six octavo volumes. It is called the *Talmud,* or "teaching," and the usual version is the Babylonian Talmud, although there also is a shorter, Jerusalem Talmud. Some parts of this were composed before the Babylonian Talmud.

POSTEXILIC THOUGHT AND PRACTICE. The period between the Exile and the beginning of the Christian era saw many changes in Judaism, some of which, however, died out or were taken up in the Christian movement. The more important are the following:

Stress on outward aspects of Judaism. The ancient custom of circumcision received new emphasis. So, too, did Sabbath observance, with stress upon refusal to travel or work on the seventh day. Ritualistic requirements for food preparation also received attention, with elaboration of dietary rules. These practices led to the growth of Jewish communities within the wider context of Babylonian culture in order that people might have ready access to properly killed meat, the services of a priest, and employment which did not require work on the Sabbath. Such concerns tended to keep Judaism strong but also to separate it from its milieu.

The synagogue. This Greek term means "assembly," and it is probable that this institution arose during the Exile. Later tradition decreed that any ten adult male Jews could organize a synagogue, both for worship and to conduct the secular affairs of a community. The synagogue became a basic institution, and after the destruction of Herod's Temple by the Romans in 70 A.D., the synagogues throughout the civilized world became centers of Judaism.

Theodicy. Why Yahweh's promises for his people went unfulfilled, while disaster after disaster occurred, became a more piercing problem after the Exile. Not only had the nation suffered humiliation, but even those individuals who sought to enact Yahweh's will by obedience to the Law met with misfortune and evil that did not substantiate the old teaching concerning rewards. The Book of Job, especially, dealt with this problem, and the author concluded that one must trust Yahweh even though immediate reward is not received. In time this led to stress on a life after death wherein rewards and punishments will compensate for the disparities of this present life.

The rise of dualistic theology. Yahweh gradually was conceived in more transcendent terms. The change of the concept of Satan from an angelic messenger to a demonic force opposed to Yahweh's rule probably was influenced by the Persian (Zoroastrian) doctrine of a Lord of Darkness. History came to be regarded by some as a battleground between Yahweh and Satan, with man caught up in the struggle.

The Kingdom of God. With stress on the future as the time when Yahweh would fulfill his purpose for Israel, the old teaching of the Day of Yahweh was reinterpreted as the hope that God would soon bring to an end the dominion of evil men and of Satan, and establish his rule "on earth as it is in heaven." Speculations articulating this hope were expressed in many forms.

The hope for a Messiah. Messiah means *the anointed one.* In early times it referred to anyone designated to be king, priest, or prophet by

Yahweh; such designation was made public by a priest's pouring oil on the head of one so designated. As the Jews looked forward to the coming of Yahweh's rule or kingdom, they speculated about the agent who would inaugurate it. Some believed that God himself would usher in his kingdom; some, that one like David of old, a "son of David," would establish it. Thus, the ancient title, Messiah, came to be the name most frequently used for the agent who would actually be sent by God when the time for the kingdom was fulfilled. From 100 B.C. to modern times various men have claimed to be the promised Messiah, or have been hailed as such by their followers.

SECTARIANISM AND THE CHRISTIAN SCHISM. After the Exile, the following important factions emerged to claim the loyalty of the Jews:

The Sadducees claimed to trace their origins back to Zadok, one of the priests of King Solomon. Although their actual origins are obscure, we know much about their activities in the Hellenistic age. The Sadducees were priestly in function and controlled the elaborate, lucrative sacrificial system of the Temple in Jerusalem. Since they were dependent upon continuing sacrifices for their livelihood, and since the number of pilgrims to Jerusalem was substantial, the Sadducees tended to favor the *status quo* and to oppose nationalistic independence movements against Rome. This group ceased to have significant influence after the Roman destruction of Herod's Temple in 70 A.D.

The Pharisees were a "puritanical" faction that insisted that the true hope of Judaism lay in obedience to the minutiae of Yahweh's will by all the people. The Pharisees interpreted the written Torah so as to show its relevance for all of life. The teachers of this movement later came to be called *Rabbis;* they were the custodians of an elaborate oral tradition which grew out of this casuistic adaptation of the Law. This oral tradition became the basis for the Mishnah and the Talmud. Although a small but militant group of Pharisees known as the Zealots believed in opposing the Roman rule by force in preparation for the Kingdom of God, most of the Pharisees trusted Yahweh to restore the fortunes of his people. They awaited the coming of the Messiah and tended to be quietistic in the struggle for national freedom. They became the dominant group after 70 A.D., the basis for Judaism as it exists today.

The Essenes were an ascetic and monastic group who had renounced the world as doomed, and waited for Yahweh to establish his kingdom.

Many scholars have identified them as the group which produced the Dead Sea Scrolls, recently discovered on the northwest shore of that sea. They died out after the Roman destruction of Jerusalem in 135 A.D.

The Christian sect first gathered around the person of a Jewish prophet, Jesus of Nazareth, who appears to have been close to the Pharisees in his teachings. After the Romans executed him (about 30 A.D.), his followers claimed that he was the long-expected Messiah or anointed one, whom Yahweh had promised to send to establish his kingdom. These people were called *Christians,* from the Greek word for Messiah, *Christos,* and they developed into an independent sect. Special Jewish observances, such as circumcision, the Sabbath, and dietary food laws, were rejected by the Christians as unimportant; they taught instead a message of salvation which was not tied to any particular group or social custom.

The Diaspora, meaning "the Dispersion," refers to the spread of Judaism beyond the borders of Palestine. It began as early as the destruction of the Northern Kingdom by the Assyrians in 721 B.C. and has had a continuous history. Many Jews fled to Egypt and other adjacent countries to escape the Babylonian Exile, establishing Jewish communities wherever they settled. These communities were vigorous and influential, producing translations of the Hebrew Bible, especially into Greek, spreading Judaism with missionary zeal, and raising the moral level of the ancient world. They not only helped Judaism to survive the final loss of their homeland when the Romans drove the Jews out of Palestine in 135 A.D., but also contributed converts to the amazing spread of early Christianity.

RABBINIC JUDAISM'S WORLD VIEW. Rabbi means chief or teacher, and refers to the religious leader who took the place of priest and prophet. After 135 A.D. the rabbis inherited the role of the Pharisees and were the chiefs of the synagogues who were learned in the Law. They preserved the oral tradition and applied Mishnaic and Talmudic teachings to daily life. The religious point of view which they represented remains essentially the position of Orthodox Judaism to this day. In the following breakdown of this theology, stress is placed upon change from the classical position before the Exile.

The cosmos. The concept of the three-level universe created by God underwent transformation, especially in the description of the supernatural. The underground Sheol became a place of punishment; the abode of the righteous was moved to Heaven, the dwelling of God.

Deity. Yahweh as creator, judge, and savior is now opposed by Satan, a created being who is in revolt against his creator. God has his angels; the Devil his demons. Belief in an expected supernatural representative of God, the Messiah, who would inaugurate God's kingdom, became normative.

Man. Although man is God's creation and therefore intrinsically good, he is endowed with two principles or tendencies: a good impulse and an evil impulse. Each struggles to control man's desires and choices. In this sense, man participates in the cosmic struggle between God and Satan.

Man's plight. God's creation has gone astray because of Satan's rebellion and the disobedience of men. Wilful neglect of God's law as revealed through Moses brings evil upon mankind. In this present world, therefore, God's power to help is frustrated and the result is misery and conflict.

Salvation. The plight of both individual man and society can be alleviated by strict obedience to the Torah. The disasters of 587 B.C. and of 135 A.D. were attributed to failure to follow the Torah. The rabbis sought to "build a fence around the Torah" by defining the ideal behavior for every detail of life in terms of their interpretations of the commandments of the Torah. The Mishnah and Talmud are monuments to this effort. Since God had found it necessary to punish the Jews in the past for failure to obey, they sought to prevent a recurrence by insuring that God's will for every contingency was clearly known.

Conduct. Rabbinic ethics involved detailed obedience to the Torah. But the "law of the heart" meant that such obedience must be total, involving the inner man as well as the outer. The notion that Christianity moved beyond Judaism in this area is based on misinterpretation of New Testament attacks on the Pharisees. Actually, the rabbinic ethic was absolute in its demands. The sanction, the motivation for such high morality, was to fulfill the Torah and to please God, the creator and Lord of life.

Destiny. The centuries-long delay in the coming of God's kingdom, and constant disillusionment—for the obedient were mistreated and killed and nonbelievers ruled the righteous—led to a hope for rewards in a future life. The doctrine of the resurrection of the body, perhaps derived from Persian influence, included the notion that a future life must have some continuity with the present, to permit consistent and just rewards and punishments for this present life. It also placed an emphasis upon a social destiny, not merely individual immortality, since the Messianic age involves the total man in his society. This age will come when God decides to bring an end to present history and sends his Messiah to overthrow evil and reward the righteous.

MEDIEVAL AND MODERN JUDAISM

JUDAISM AS A CULTURAL EXPRESSION. In early Christian times, Judaism continued to have a missionary emphasis, proclaiming the "One True God" and calling men to a life of ethical living in service of God as revealed in the Torah. When the Emperor Constantine made Christianity an official religion of the Roman Empire (c. 325 A.D.), Judaism began to be proscribed. As a result, Judaism turned inward, with almost complete stress upon the community and its practices. By 500 A.D. the Talmud was committed to writing and every detail of a Jew's life was prescribed by this religious law. God's will for Judaism came to be identified with the cultural expression to be found in the Talmud. To this day, the Orthodox Jew seeks to follow this same talmudic way of life, and the history of Judaism from 500 A.D. to the French Revolution involves very little in the way of religious development.

MAIMONIDES. Although most Jewish thought was restricted to applying talmudic teachings to every aspect of life, it produced one great apologist and philosopher of lasting importance, Maimonides (1135-1204). Born in Spain, he lived all his life under Muslim influence, received an excellent education in Greek and Islamic thought, and became physician at the court of the famous Egyptian Sultan, Saladin. He wrote in Arabic; his most famous contribution to Judaism was the working out of a credo, or set of thirteen beliefs, which is to this day the basis of Orthodoxy. His stress (perhaps reflecting Islamic emphasis) was upon the unity and omniscience of God, who alone is to be worshiped, upon the unchangeableness of the revelation of the Law to Moses, the greatest of all prophets, and upon the doctrine that God rewards and punishes man, as well as upon the hope for the Messiah and the belief in the resurrection of the dead. Although Judaism does not require acceptance of a creed, and Maimonides has had many critics, his succinct summary was highly influential.

THE GHETTO. This Italian word refers to districts in medieval cities to which Jews were restricted. This restriction was due in part to the desire of the Jews to follow their own talmudic way of life, but was especially due to the Christians' persecution of the Jews. (Under Islam, Judaism did not suffer as much as under Christianity.) The result was an even further intensification of the introspective tendency of Judaism, which led to such developments as the Kabbalah.

THE KABBALAH. The Hebrew term *Qabbalah* means "tradition" and designates a mystical school of thought which arose in Southern Europe in the thirteenth century. It is pantheistic in doctrine, undoubtedly influenced by neo-Platonism and Gnosticism, and teaches that there is a hidden god behind the creator God of Genesis. This movement illustrates a tendency in all religions: religious persons, impatient with mere form and legalism, attempt to express basic desires for the experience of union with the deity, or at least of feeling themselves part of the cosmic whole. Although the meaning of the Kabbalah is obscure, its widespread influence illustrates the danger of describing Judaism as simply a cultural expression of the Talmud.

THE ENLIGHTENMENT. In the eighteenth century, Judaism began to emerge from the Ghetto and to share in the revolutionary movements to promote learning and equality which were shaking Europe. Moses Mendelssohn (1729-86), the German philosopher, was the most influential leader in the *Haskalah,* or movement of enlightenment. The French Revolution helped to level both the physical and religious barriers of the Ghetto. The pent-up dynamism of Judaism burst out into Europe and America; Jewish thinkers, artists, and educators have contributed far more to the development of Western culture than their numbers would lead one to expect.

CONTEMPORARY JUDAISM. Events in the past century have led to a regrouping of the tenets of Judaism. The large-scale exodus of Jews from Russia, Central Europe, and Germany to the Americas before World War I had shifted the numerical strength so that it approached a balance between Europe and the New World. Then the hideous atrocities of the German Nazi regime, with the slaughter of at least six million European Jews, made the United States the new center of Judaism.

In 1948 the establishment of the country of Israel by a United Nations decree created a homeland for dispossessed and persecuted Jews. Because of the continued persecution of Jews in Soviet Russia, for many of them Israel represents the only hope for security. The modern State of Israel is an interesting mixture of secular nationalism and Orthodox piety. The economic development of the country has been amazing, but the vigor of the young nation is partially offset by the fact that it is set in the midst of the Islamic world.

In America, which is the present numerical and financial center of Judaism, there are three main branches of the religion. The Orthodox group attempts to follow the talmudic teachings on kosher rules, Sabbath observance, and avoidance of too much mixing with the "outside" world.

Reform Judaism essentially seeks to adapt itself to the ways of the society in which it exists. In America this means laying aside most talmudic practices, often even changing the Sabbath service to Sunday, calling synagogues "temples," and stressing belief in God and ethical living.

The Conservative movement seeks to retain essential Judaism by following the set feasts, such as Passover, and reinterpreting the Law for modern times while avoiding the tendencies to assimilation of Reform Judaism. The Conservative movement has a vigorous intellectual leadership, and its concern to relate religion to life has much in common with that of the neo-orthodox movement in Christianity.

With the State of Israel as a haven for persecuted and uprooted Jews, and with the greatest number of Jews (over five and one-half million) concentrated in the United States of America, Judaism today faces an open future.

Chapter Five

ZOROASTRIANISM

Zoroastrianism survives today primarily among the community of Parsis (Persians) in the Bombay area of India. For our purposes, this religion would be little more than a museum piece were it not that Zoroastrian theology greatly influenced the Judaeo-Christian tradition, both directly and indirectly. This is especially true in respect to the concepts of dualistic forces of good and evil (God and the Devil), of a coming kingdom of god, a future savior, and bodily resurrection. For historical reasons, therefore, a brief summary of this religion is essential.

THE LIFE OF ZOROASTER. Zoroaster is the Greek rendering of the Old Persian name, *Zarathustra.* He was born in eastern Persia (modern Iran), but little is known about his life; even the dates of his activity are uncertain. One school of thought places it around 1000 B.C.; the usual date given is 660 B.C., but increasing evidence supports a date for his ministry in the first half of the sixth century B.C.

Although it is customary to show how Zoroastrian thought influenced the Jews during the Persian rule of Palestine (539-331 B.C.), it is also interesting to note the many similarities between earlier Hebrew prophecy and the teachings of Zoroaster. At about the age of thirty, Zoroaster began to proclaim "One True God" and to attack the religious beliefs and practices of his countrymen. He claimed to be a spokesman for the god Ahura Mazdah. Zoroaster announced that Ahura Mazdah had revealed himself to him and had charged him to proclaim his message to the world. At first, Zoroaster had little success with his message in his home territory; later he moved to northeast Iran where he was championed by a local king named Hystaspes. Here he was more successful and converted many to his new religion.

Zoroaster lived when the pastoral life of Persia was giving way to a more settled agricultural economy. He opposed the more barbaric practices of the nomadic peoples and advocated the pursuit of agriculture and the spread of settled life. Essentially his message stressed the call to serve Ahura Mazdah, the Wise Lord, and to renounce loyalty to all other spiritual beings, especially the Lord of Evil, Angra Mainyu. Zoroaster also opposed the cultic practices of his day, which involved bloody sacrifices and drunkenness, much as Amos and Hosea, a few centuries earlier in Palestine, had opposed the cult of Baal. Apparently he was a practicing monotheist in the same way that Moses was, i.e., not denying the existence of other gods, but insisting on the necessity of siding with the true god against all other gods.

We know that by the time of Darius I, the Great (522-486 B.C.), Ahura Mazdah was claimed as the Great God of the Persians, and that this religion continued to have much influence in succeeding centuries. Literary sources preserving the thought of Zoroaster are late, however, and their meaning is often obscure. Very little is known with certainty about the actual position of Zoroaster on crucial theological teachings.

THE SCRIPTURES OF ZOROASTRIANISM. The most important Zoroastrian scripture is known as the *Avesta,* a name which denotes the language in which it is written. This language was akin to the early Vedic language of the Aryan invaders of India, who came of the same stock as the Iranians. In its present form the Avesta dates from the Sassanian dynasty (c. 226-651 A.D.) when there was an official revival of Zoroastrianism in Persia. It consists of three main divisions:

The Yasna, or liturgy. This section contains seventeen poems or hymns scattered through the text—the famous *Gathas* ascribed to Zoroaster as prophetic utterances. Their form and language are archaic and bristle with difficulties for the translator; in fact, the bulk of them are either obscure or impossible to translate without ambiguity. These hymns constitute the closest approximation to the actual message of Zoroaster.

The Yashts, which consist of hymns addressed to various angelic beings and gods as part of the sacrificial ceremony.

The Vendidad (translated to mean "The Law against the Demons") is a compendium of laws and mythology.

Pahlavi texts. The Sassanian orthodoxy which prevailed up to the time of the Muslim eclipse of Zoroastrianism in Persia produced a voluminous literature in the Middle Persian dialect of Pahlavi, akin to the language of the Parthians to the northeast of Iran. This literature gives full expression to much that is implied in early Zoroastrian thought, but because it is relatively late, it has been of only secondary interest to Western scholars.

THE WORLD VIEW OF EARLY ZOROASTRIANISM. Although it has proved difficult to ascertain Zoroaster's own thought, we shall outline the basic world view ascribed to him and then discuss the treatment later accorded his message.

The cosmos. Underlying the prophet's message appears a fairly uncomplicated conception of the universe. As has been true for most reformers, Zoroaster did not speculate about the nature of ultimate reality or about details of cosmogony. His cosmos consisted of three levels: heaven, earth, and an underworld. This was created by the deity, Ahura Mazdah, and was under his control. With this concept of creation is joined the concept of time and space as limiting factors for the created world. All this is similar to the basic world view of the Bible, especially as found in the early chapters of Genesis.

Deity. The chief deity was Ahura Mazdah, the Wise Lord, god of light and truth, who revealed himself to Zoroaster and commissioned him to be his prophet or spokesman. Ahura Mazdah is creator of the universe, the one who will be the final judge and redeemer of history. Meanwhile, another force calling for the loyalty of men is at work in the world. This is Angra Mainyu (or Ahriman) who is the antithesis of Ahura Mazdah. He is Lord of Darkness and of Lies, and is sometimes referred to as the twin of Ahura Mazdah.

How a creator god can be lord of all, and yet allow a force of evil to oppose him, is a problem faced but not resolved by Zoroastrian thought. One suggestion is that both gods, good and evil, were produced from the interaction of chaos and time. Another is that Angra Mainyu, like the Devil of Christianity, was a created being who rebelled against his creator. But true faith holds that, in the cosmic struggle in which the two deities are engaged for control of the world, Ahura Mazdah will surely win.

Each of these deities has a group of helpers akin to the angels and demons of late biblical thought. Ahura Mazdah is assigned five, or sometimes six *Amesha Spentas* which at first may have represented the most important attributes of his being, but were later personified as subsidiary deities. These are *Vohu Mano,* Good Mind; *Asha,* Righteousness; *Kshathra,* Sovereignty; *Armaiti,* Devotion; *Hauvatat,* Welfare; and *Ameretat,* Immortality.

The evil counterparts of the Amesha Spentas are the *daevas,* a term (deva) which was used for the gods themselves in the Vedic religion of India. These daevas probably are the other gods of the Iranian tribes of Zoroaster's time who were labeled by him false gods, much as Moses and the Hebrew prophets labeled the gods of Egypt and Palestine false. All who opposed Ahura Mazdah were listed as siding with Angra Mainyu, so that evil beasts and faithless men also were counted among the minions of the Devil.

One other important divine being in the Zoroastrian mythology is the *Shaoshyant,* the figure of an expected savior, on the order of the concept of the "son of man" in the Judaic lore of New Testament times. He is to come in judgment and to inaugurate the kingdom of heaven, which represents the rule of Ahura Mazdah.

Man. According to the Zoroastrian doctrine of man, he has been created by Ahura Mazdah and is responsible to his creator's demands. Man has both a body and a spirit or soul. As a created being, he can side with good beings, who are already obedient, such as angels and dogs (the dog appears frequently in Zoroastrian mythology), or with Angra Mainyu. This means that man has freedom of choice, or he could not choose between good and evil. That the doctrine of rebirth, which was taught by this time in the Upanishads of India was neglected, lends some support to the position that rebirth is peculiarly an Indian notion, rather than Aryan in origin. In Zoroastrianism, man has but one life in which to determine his destiny. This doctrine emphasizes moral struggle, rather than the search for knowledge, as the chief end of man.

Man's plight. If men and animals are created by a good deity, why then are there evil men and beasts? Probably Zoroaster himself began with the simple premise that there was rebellion against that true god whose will he proclaimed. But the mythology of the late Pahlavi texts tells how the first couple were led astray (like Adam and Eve) by evil thoughts and began to worship the daevas rather than Ahura Mazdah.

The present plight of man, however, is more clearly explained. It is caused by disobedience to the will of Ahura Mazdah as proclaimed by his prophet and even by active rebellion against the will of the god. Man is responsible for his disobedience and therefore guilty of self-will.

Salvation. Man's salvation is to be found in obedience to the will of Ahura Mazdah as it was revealed and taught by his spokesman or prophet, Zoroaster. This obedience is neither legalistic nor mechanical, but positive. Man is to work with his god and to combat the forces of evil wherever they are found. Some scholars are of the opinion that Zoroaster thought that he might be able to rally men under Ahura Mazdah's banner to build a kingdom of righteousness during his lifetime. In any case this religion, like Judaism, Christianity, and Islam, calls upon man to choose sides in the cosmic struggle between good and evil, right and wrong, to affirm and improve the world, not to deny and escape it. The decision to side with Ahura Mazdah against all opposition is, of course, predicated upon the conviction that Zoroaster really does speak in the name of the true god and that his cause will be victorious in the end.

Conduct. The sanction or motivation for right conduct is the need to please Ahura Mazdah; as well as the desire to be a soldier in his army, fighting against evil. The greatest virtue is truth. The other three cardinal virtues are good thoughts, good words, and good deeds. A man is to treat his neighbor with justice and equity; he is also to fight all enemies of the true religion as though they were his own enemies. Some of Zoroaster's specific injunctions reflect the background of his stand, opposing the nomad and eulogizing the settled husbandman. Thus it is virtuous to spread agriculture; early rising and hard work are praised, and the dog (as protector of property) is treated as a partner of man.

Destiny. Each of the four monotheistic religions teaches that what happens after death is in the hands of its god. A man chooses to serve or to disobey his god, but the final results of this choice will not be realized until after death, unless, of course, one's god chooses to inaugurate his kingdom now. The righteous Zoroastrian, therefore, will be rewarded with a place in a heaven where he will be with Ahura Mazdah and will share in his blessed existence. Those who have chosen to follow the lead of Angra Mainyu have been led astray by lies and enticing promises, and after death will suffer terrible torments in an underworld. At death, each is judged and transported to his deserved abode. The famous myth of the Chinvat Bridge tells of how the righteous will pass easily over a deep chasm, while the wicked will find the bridge as narrow as a razor's edge and will fall headlong into hell.

A kind of universalism is implied in the teaching of a final judgment. When the Shaoshyant comes to inaugurate the Kingdom of Righteousness there will be a resurrection and a final judgment. At the end of a cosmic year, lasting some twelve thousand earthly years, there is to be a general resurrection of both the good and the bad, and all will pass through a purging stream. To the souls of the righteous it will be as warm milk, to the wicked like molten metal. All sin will be burned away by the stream and all mankind will be forever with Ahura Mazdah.

The student of biblical eschatology will note many parallels between this presentation of Zoroastrian thought and postexilic Jewish and early Christian eschatology. How much one has influenced the other and which elements are originally biblical or Persian cannot be decided. It is undoubtedly true that Persian rule over the Jews influenced Jewish theology, as witness the eschatology of the Pseudepigrapha, including the Dead Sea Scrolls or, more pertinently, the New Testament book of The Revelation to John.

ZOROASTRIANISM IN HISTORY. Toward the end of Zoroaster's prophetic ministry, Cyrus the Great created the Persian empire by overthrowing the Median rule of Astyages. Cyrus rapidly expanded his new kingdom and in 539 B.C. conquered Babylon. Under Cyrus, the Jews, as well as other national groups, were allowed to return to their homeland and to re-establish their religion, although under Persian political control. It is probable that during this period of tolerance Judaism borrowed many theological concepts from Zoroastrian thought.

In 525, Cyrus's son, Cambyses, conquered Egypt; then, after a brief period of confusion, Darius Hystaspis, or Darius I, became the new Persian emperor. His long rule (522-486) involved unsuccessful attempts to extend the empire into Europe; he lost the battle of Marathon, 490 B.C. His successor, Xerxes, suffered a decisive naval defeat at Salamis. It has been suggested that had the Persians been successful in their attempts to rule Europe, the West might have become Zoroastrian rather than Christian. But this did not occur, and in 331 B.C. Alexander the Great took over the Persian empire. After the breakup of Alexander's empire, the Parthians from Bactria ruled Persia until 212 A.D.

At this time, the New Persian empire was founded by Artaxerxes, who began the Sassanian line. During the Sassanian period, Zoroastrianism became the state religion and experienced a genuine renascence. The Pahlavi texts, which include much theological and metaphysical speculation, were composed at this time. But in 637 A.D., the rapidly expanding Islamic movement reached Persia, and Muslim rule proscribed Zoroastrianism. Since the Muslims regarded the Zoroastrians as a "people of a book," or believers in prophetic religion, they were treated with tolerance. The restrictions in the area of politics and economics which were placed upon non-Muslims, however, took their toll, and Persia soon became dominantly Muslim.

In the eighth century, a group of Zoroastrians fled to western India, where they became known as *Parsis,* from the word for Persia. Through the centuries, they accommodated their practices to those of the Hindus around them, but in the last century, there has been a revival of interest in their religion. Under the influence of Western scholars, the Parsis reformed some of their practices. One practice for which they are still famous is based on the early Zoroastrian teaching of the sacredness of fire and earth, which led to the prohibition of both cremation and burial of the dead. Instead, the Parsis place a corpse on a platform in a hollow tower and wait for the vultures to clean the bones, which are removed at intervals for special burying.

Today, the Parsis are concentrated around Bombay, where they number over 125,000 people. They are a respected and influential group whose numbers are increasing at the present time.

Chapter Six

CHRISTIANITY

Christianity is a syncretistic religion, a mixture of several traditions. Judaism, out of which Christianity arose, already had a mixed heritage, including Egyptian, Babylonian, and Canaanite influences, and was further enriched by Zoroastrian and Hellenistic contacts. In the early Church, this Jewish heritage was combined with the equally diverse Greek world view. In fact, the complexities of Christian origins have been the despair of historians, and make any descriptive account of the beginnings of the Church an arbitrary ordering of essential data.

THE JUDAIC BACKGROUND

REVEALED RELIGION. Christianity is a revealed religion like Judaism, out of which it arose. To the Christian, the Jewish scriptures are the Old Testament: a pre-Christian testament or covenant which the God of the Jews has made with man. In this old covenant, Yahweh made his will known to his chosen people in several ways. One was through the teachings of Moses, the founder of Judaism, and through the Law which developed and bore his name. The stress on Yahweh's will, as made known through the Law, meant that the priestly group concerned itself with ritual, sacrifice, and the more formal aspects of Judaism, even though justice and love were not ignored. The sages of Judaism, for their part, interpreted Yahweh's will in terms of *wisdom*. Basically, this was a prudential ethic, stressing the *fear* of the Lord, as we can see in the Book of Proverbs.

Prophetic revelation also stressed ethical concerns, but these were placed in the context of obedience to the will of Yahweh as made known through his "spokesmen," the prophets. The prophets had proclaimed a double message: a message of doom upon a sinful nation for its failure to repent and turn back to Yahweh, and a message of hope. This message included the promise that some day God would restore the fortunes of his people even though their history was primarily one of subjugation and oppression at the hands of Egyptians, Babylonians, Assyrians, Persians, Greeks, and finally, Romans.

The hope for the nation was expressed variously, sometimes in contradictory ways, but the faith that Yahweh would fulfill his promise was always affirmed. Sometimes the coming of an ideal king, who would overthrow the enemy by military might and restore the nation to its greatness during the reigns of David and Solomon, was predicted. Sometimes the hope was given a more spiritual meaning, with a stress on peace and righteousness instead of national power. For some, the coming change of fortune involved materialistic rewards in this life; others looked for a radical transformation of the earth by the bringing of God's heaven to earth. But for God to accomplish his purpose, he needed some agent to effect his work.

THE MESSIANIC HOPE. The term Messiah, meaning "the anointed," was used often in the Old Testament to refer to anyone chosen by Yahweh, or designated as a religious leader by ritual anointing with oil. Thus Saul became Yahweh's Messiah when Samuel anointed him king; so did David and all the other Hebrew kings. The term came to have the meaning of one elected or chosen by Yahweh to represent him on earth. The hope for a future Messiah therefore meant the hope for one who would be designated by Yahweh to bring in his kingdom. Again, the term *son of David* might refer to the hope that Yahweh would send "one like David of old" to restore the fortunes of his people. In each case, of course, the content of that Messianic hope would depend upon the particular emphasis given to it, whether materialistic, spiritual, or otherworldly.

END OF PROPHECY; APOCALYPTIC WRITINGS. In the time of Jesus, Jewish tradition held that Yahweh had ceased to speak directly through his prophets, and that his will was now to be found only in the earlier records of Torah and prophecy. It was accepted dogma that, since the time of Ezra in 444 B.C., pronouncements of doom and of hope in the name of Yahweh no longer were divinely inspired. God would again speak directly through prophecy only after the dawn of the new age. But there had developed a form of literary expression known as apocalyptic (revealed), which continued to proclaim God's care for his chosen people and had a wide following. The prime example of such writings is the Book of Daniel, wherein the author proclaims his faith that God will aid his people against the Hellenistic oppressors under

Antiochus IV (175-163 B.C.). The success of the Maccabean revolt in 168 B.C. helped to strengthen the faith and hope of the Jews that Yahweh had not forgotten his promises. This apocalyptic hope, which would be fulfilled by world cataclysms, angels, and cosmic judgments, kept alive the vital concept that God continued to have a special message for his people in each age.

JESUS AND THE BEGINNINGS OF CHRISTIANITY

JOHN THE BAPTIST. The story of the ministry of Jesus begins about 28 A.D., when Palestine was under the rule of the Romans. The people suffered under heavy taxation, and longed for freedom and peace. In the midst of this oppression John, called the Baptist, began to preach, announcing that the end of one age had come and that God was about to intervene in the affairs of man. He warned his hearers to renounce their disobedient ways and turn back to God. He introduced the ritual of baptism, the sign of a desire to repent and prepare for the imminent judgment of God.

One of John's hearers was Jesus, who came from the town of Nazareth in Galilee. He accepted the rite of baptism and, soon after, underwent a time of testing in the wilderness. Tradition tells us that Jesus was tempted thrice: he was tempted to present God's kingdom as of this world, to lead the people by satisfying their physical needs; he was tempted to gain followers by the use of miracles; and he was tempted to forsake obedience to God for the sake of worldly power (Matt. 4:1-11). But he refused, insisting on the need to serve God and God alone.

Shortly after Jesus' baptism, John the Baptist was arrested. Jesus himself then began to proclaim that God was about to establish his rule on earth. "Now after John was arrested, Jesus came into Galilee, preaching the gospel of God, and saying, 'The time is fulfilled, and the kingdom of God is at hand; repent, and believe in the gospel'" (Mark 1:14-15).

JESUS AS PROPHET. Both John and Jesus spoke as prophets, implying that the time of prophetic silence had passed and that with the dawn of the new age God was once more making his will known through human spokesmen. Jesus' proclamation stressed that the long-awaited Day of the Lord was about to dawn on men, ushering in the rule of God, his "kingdom." He stressed that the kingdom was near at hand; that the need to prepare for it was urgent, since with it would come judgment upon men's disobedience. His message called upon his hearers to make sacrifices, even though this might mean renouncing everything of value in this world, in order to be ready for God's rule. At the same time, this message of the imminence of judgment and of radical renunciation was accompanied by words of hope in which forgiveness and fulfilment were stressed. "Blessed are you that hunger now, for you shall be satisfied" (Luke 6:21). God's kingdom would be a blessing to the poor and oppressed who were obedient, just as surely as it would destroy the power of the mighty of this world. Jesus also voiced the apocalyptic faith that God would overcome all the forces of evil, not merely the kingdoms of this world, but also the dominion of the Devil. A typical apocalyptic saying is found in Luke 10:17-20:

The seventy returned with joy, saying, "Lord, even the demons are subject to us in your name!" And he said to them, "I saw Satan fall like lightning from heaven. Behold, I have given you authority to tread upon serpents and scorpions, and over all the power of the enemy; and nothing shall hurt you. Nevertheless do not rejoice in this, that the spirits are subject to you; but rejoice that your names are written in heaven."

JESUS' ETHICS. One of the important aspects of Jesus' preaching of the coming kingdom of God was his stress upon the ethical demands this imminent event made upon his hearers. Although the content of Jesus' teachings was basically Judaic, the sanctions for his ethics were radical. In different ways he showed what it would mean to obey God absolutely, to be under his rule, to be a citizen of the kingdom of God.

You have heard that it was said to the men of old, "You shall not kill; and whoever kills shall be liable to judgment." But I say to you that every one who is angry with his brother shall be liable to judgment; whoever insults his brother shall be liable to the council, and whoever says "You fool!" shall be liable to the hell of fire (Matt. 5:21-22).

You have heard that it was said, "You shall not commit adultery." But I say to you that every one who looks at a woman lustfully has already committed adultery with her in his heart (Matt. 5:27-28).

The parables of Jesus and his other ethical teachings appear basically to be adjunct to his proclamation of the imminence of God's judgment. God is to be obeyed as sovereign Lord in every area of life, in preparation for God's coming and in illustration of what life in his kingdom will be like.

JESUS' MISSION. Jesus' ministry was brief, probably less than one year in duration, if we follow the evidence of Mark's Gospel. He gathered a group of disciples to work with him and proclaim the coming kingdom. They followed him as a true prophet of God. Jesus' own conception of his relationship to the coming rule of God is difficult to ascertain, but it appears that he rejected any notion that he would be a leader of a military or nationalistic attempt to throw off the Roman yoke and establish God's rule by force. He called upon his hearers to seek to obey God's will even if this might mean suffering and death.

After a brief ministry, he was arrested by the Jewish authorities as one who opposed the customs of the day. He was crucified by the Romans at the time of the Jewish Passover as a troublemaker and potential revolutionary, probably in the year 30 A.D.

THE RESURRECTION. Shortly after the execution of Jesus, his disciples began to proclaim that God had raised him from the dead. His resurrection was hailed as the beginning of the new age, the kingdom of God, that Jesus had announced. He was the first to be resurrected, and before long, he would return to judge the world as God's representative, after the dead had all been raised up to participate in a final judgment. The resurrection of Jesus was said to be proof that he was actually the long-awaited Messiah.

THE EARLIEST CHRISTIAN COMMUNITY. The new movement which began in Palestine soon spread among Jews of the Hellenistic communities outside the Jewish homeland. Very quickly, several characteristics of the Christian community began to crystallize and a distinctive Jewish sect came into being.

Jesus as the Jewish Messiah. The first characteristic of the new sect was the belief that Jesus truly was the Messiah. To this day, the basic difference between Jew and Christian is that the latter claims that the Messiah has already come in the person of Jesus, while the former still awaits the coming of his Messiah.

The Holy Spirit as a proof of faith in the resurrection. Judaism held that Yahweh's spirit had not spoken directly to men since the time of Ezra, but the Christians claimed that once again God's spirit was active in prophecy. The experience of possession by God's spirit was proof to the Christian that the new age had dawned with Jesus' resurrection (Acts 2:14-21).

Jesus as Lord. As Christianity moved from Palestine into Greek areas, one of the titles given to Jesus was *Lord* (Greek, *Kurios*). In the mystery religions of the Hellenistic age, the god was called "Lord"; this title meant that the devotee was the god's slave and the god would protect and save his servants, and guide them through the doors of death to immortality. So Jesus came to be presented to the non-Jewish world as a risen Lord rather than merely a Jewish Messiah. The new movement, which at first had comprised only Jews, soon attracted many Gentiles, and when these Gentile converts received the gift of the Holy Spirit, this was taken as proof of their right to join the movement. This development led to the final separation of the Christian Church from its parent religion, Judaism.

THE CHRISTIAN SCRIPTURES. Jesus himself left no writings, so that all that is known about his life and teachings was preserved by his disciples. At first it was believed that Jesus, the heavenly Son of Man, would soon return to judge the world, so the early Christians proclaimed the message (good news or gospel) of Jesus as risen Lord orally; they were little concerned to record it in writing. The earliest Christian writings that have been preserved are the letters of the Apostle Paul (died c. 65 A.D.). The second generation of Christians produced further documents, many of which have been preserved as the Christian Scriptures, known as the New Testament. They all are in Greek and date from 50 A.D. to 150 A.D.

At first, the only sacred writings were those of Judaism, which for Jesus and the early Church included only the Law and the Prophets. Since Christianity spread rapidly among the Jews of the Diaspora, the Septuagint, or Greek version of the Old Testament, which included the Apocrypha, soon was used.

The New Testament. By 367 A.D. the group of early Christian writings ascribed to disciples of Jesus, to the Apostle Paul, and his associate, Luke, was complete. This New Testament, or record of the covenant between God and the new Israel, the Christian Church, all Christian communions accept as authoritative. It consists of twenty-seven writings, listed here by types and approximately in chronological order.

THE LETTERS OF PAUL. The fourteen writings ascribed to Paul are addressed to churches or to individuals. Thirteen bear his name and, of these, liberal scholarship accepts nine or ten as actually by Paul. These are Romans; 1 and 2 Corinthians; Galatians; Philippians; Colossians; 1 and 2 Thessalonians; Philemon; and, some would add, Ephesians. Three, called *Pastorals* because they are addressed to pastors of churches, reflect later thought and often are labeled *deutero-Pauline*. These three are 1 and 2 Timothy, and Titus. The fourteenth letter, ascribed to Paul by tradition, is Hebrews. Actually, we do not know who wrote it.

THE FOUR GOSPELS. These are, in probable chronological order, Mark, dated about 70 A.D., attributed to a certain John Mark; Matthew, dated about 85 A.D., attributed to Jesus' disciple by that name; Luke, usually dated about 95 A.D., attributed to a friend of Paul; and John, dated after 100 A.D., and attributed to a disciple of Jesus.

THE BOOK OF ACTS, the only New Testament history, is by the same writer as the Gospel of Luke.

SEVEN "CATHOLIC" OR GENERAL WRITINGS addressed to the Church in general or to unknown Christians: 1 and 2 Peter, probably later than the disciple Peter, who died c. 65 A.D.; James, ascribed to the brother of Jesus; 1, 2, and 3 John, letters by an unknown elder of the primitive Church, but linked to the Gospel of John; and Jude, a short apocalyptic writing.

THE REVELATION TO JOHN, an apocalyptic writing, thought to have been composed about 96 A.D. to encourage Christians suffering persecution under the Emperor Domitian.

The Apostolic Fathers. These important writings are from the same period as much of the New Testament but are not accepted as canonical, since they are not attributed to the earliest apostles. They are a prime source for our knowledge of the thought of the early Church.

THE WORLD VIEW OF EARLY CHRISTIANITY. From these sources, we will describe early Christian theology. Its scheme of salvation is based upon Jewish presuppositions, but there are several important additions.

The cosmos. The God of Abraham, Moses, and the prophets is creator of the universe, judge, and savior. But the cosmos is in need of redemption: this present evil age is about to be ended and a new age, the kingdom of God, is to replace it.

Deity. The God of Judaism is sovereign, but he is opposed by Satan, the Devil, who personifies rebellion against God's will on the part of spiritual forces. God has angels (messengers) to aid him in ruling the universe; the Devil has demons to work for his cause.

The Holy Spirit, representing an aspect of Yahweh's power at work in the world, is an early Christian concept. The New Testament book of *The Acts of the Apostles* (chapter 2) tells how the first Christians received the gift of God's Holy Spirit at Pentecost, the ancient Jewish feast honoring the giving of the Law, the basis of the old covenant, to Moses. In this story the Holy Spirit replaces the Law as the organ of God's revelation for the Christian.

Belief in the Holy Spirit was linked with faith in the resurrection, and early teaching represents Jesus, the risen Lord, as also embodying an aspect of God's saving power. Paul describes Jesus as "designated Son of God in power according to the Spirit of holiness by his resurrection from the dead, Jesus Christ our Lord" (Rom. 1:4). Many other New Testament passages ascribe divinity to Jesus and link him with the various activities of God, namely, as aiding in creation, as judge, and as divine savior.

Man. Man is God's creation, free to obey or to disobey his creator. He has a single life in which to make this final decision, but its significance is cosmic and eternal. The New Testament has no consistent description of the nature of man, using such terms as body, strength, soul, spirit, mind, and conscience. The Hebrew teaching that man is a unity of soul and body and neither is complete without the other is retained, but the earliest sources also reflect the Greek notion of the body as evil and the soul as good.

Man's plight. The Old Testament teaching that man's plight was caused by disobedience to God's will is accepted. Man also is in need of help, of redemption, from the various forces which would enslave and destroy him. Death, fear, physical distress, hopelessness, and his own selfishness and lusts all hold man in bondage. In addition, man is confronted by such supernatural forces as the Devil, sin and death, against whose strength his own power is ineffectual.

Salvation. Since man is caught in a struggle which will engulf him unless he receives supernatural help, his salvation is only to be found in faith in Christ; that is, in acceptance of Jesus' resurrection from the dead as proof that God has power over the forces of sin and death. Just as Jewish faith is predicated on the fact of God's saving help at the Exodus from Egypt, so the Christian finds his faith in the resurrection. Faith in Jesus as Christ and risen Lord makes available to the believer the power of the Holy Spirit, through which a mortal, in bondage to fear and hopelessness, is freed and becomes triumphant, even over death itself.

To participate in that new life which Christians claimed they received by the power of the Holy Spirit, a believer had to confess that for him Jesus was Christ and Lord. He then received baptism, which was a ritual induction into the community of believers and was expected to insure the gift of the Spirit. As a member of the Church (the Greek term is *ekklesia,* meaning "gathering") the convert shared in a sacramental meal known as the *Eucharist* (Greek, "to give thanks"). This common meal was in memory of Jesus' last meal with his disciples and also anticipated Jesus' return to inaugurate God's kingdom by eating this "last supper" with his faithful followers.

Conduct. Christianity inherited the high ethic of Judaism, and added to it many ethical teachings of the Stoics and other Hellenistic philosophers. But the motivation for ethical living was based upon faith in Jesus Christ. Since God offers forgiveness to those who believe and thereby adopts them as his sons, the Christian should live a life of obedience out of gratitude to God and also as proof of the fact of his faith. This life of obedience is possible with the help of the Holy Spirit, the true guide for Christian living. The early Church also collected many of the teachings of Jesus for use in instructing converts in ethical living; in time, these teachings became normative for most Christians. Thus, although Jesus appears to have opposed legalism, his own words eventually became the basis for a Christian legalism.

Destiny. Jewish and Christian thought about destiny is predicated upon the belief that just as God is creator of the world and lord of history so, too, the future is under his control. No single position is to be found, however, concerning the destiny of the individual or of the future of society. Early Christian thought on this subject is further complicated by the addition of new elements from the Hellenistic world into which Christianity moved. As early as the time when Paul was writing, the Jewish concept of the resurrection of the body was blended with the Greek idea of the immortality of the soul. This resulted in the interesting notion of the resurrection of a spiritual body, implying that life after death will be both social (ethical) and spiritual in nature.

Although Jesus was proclaimed as the long-awaited Jewish Messiah, he also is to return again as Son of Man, when the dead will be resurrected. At this time he is to judge the world and inaugurate the kingdom of God by bringing God's rule to earth. Along with this teaching of the Parousia, or second coming of Christ, is the promise of heaven as a place of immediate reward for the faithful after death, and of hell as a place of punishment for the wicked and nonbelievers.

CHRISTIANITY AS A MISSIONARY RELIGION

As a missionary religion, Christianity has spread around the world, especially into western Asia, Europe, North and South America, Australia, and much of Africa. It now claims some 850,000,000 members. Here we shall outline the missionary dynamics which help to explain why Christianity has spread beyond the land of its origin, and yet has retained its essential nature through the centuries.

ESSENTIALS OF A MISSIONARY RELIGION. A religion must possess three distinctive characteristics in order to succeed as a missionary movement without dissipating its energies or splintering when it collides with other religions and cultures. These three characteristics are universality, continuity, and adaptability.

Universality. The message of the religion must be available to anyone. A missionary religion must transcend all human barriers, such as birth, race, sex, and nationality. Its message must offer help and meaning in life to all mankind and to every individual; otherwise it cannot replace the religion followed by prospective converts.

Continuity, the second requirement, has two aspects. The first is a link with the past. A missionary religion must be based on a tradition which gives it authority; it must have the soil of an established culture for its propagation. Constant factors which will hold the religion together as it spreads out into strange lands form the second aspect of continuity.

Adaptability is the third necessary characteristic. Though a missionary religion must have definite continuity as it moves out into wider geographic areas, it must also be able to adapt itself to new situations or its strangeness will cause it to be rejected by potential converts. As a subsidiary consideration, adaptability includes the need for a degree of relevance to concerns of this world, such as the economic and political problems of society.

CHRISTIANITY'S UNIVERSALITY. The Roman Empire of the first century A.D. was the scene of intense religious activity. There probably were many more Jews living outside Palestine than in that land. The religious message of Stoicism was spreading rapidly among the soldiers who had been uprooted from the stable life of village or farm and sent to far-off places, to face death, or to spend years with little or no hope of returning to their ancestral homes. The mystery religions were active also, offering the promise of immortality to those who would accept initiation into the secret cults. Yet in competition with all these religions and cults, Christianity triumphed and within three centuries became the official religion of the Roman Empire.

As has been indicated, syncretism is characteristic of Christianity. In its early history Jewish and Hellenistic elements mixed, fusing the strengths of each. The creator god of Judaism offered present guidance and future immortality to all who would accept Jesus as Messiah and risen Lord. Both Jew and Gentile were included in Paul's statement, "since all have sinned and fall short of the glory of God, they are justified by his grace as a gift, through the redemption which is in Christ Jesus" (Rom. 3:23-24). Paul rejected as unimportant for salvation specific requirements of the Law of Moses—circumcision, kosher regulations, and Sabbath laws. And the Christian message was all-inclusive, not restricted to men as many of the Hellenistic cults were, and as even Judaism tended to be. All, from nobleman to slave, were offered salvation. "In Christ Jesus you are all sons of God, through faith. For as many of you as were baptized into Christ have put on Christ, there is neither Jew nor Greek, there is neither slave nor free, there is neither male nor female; for you are all one in Christ Jesus" (Gal. 3:26-28).

Those two things most important to man were included: the Jewish emphasis upon ethical living in this present life was presented as obedience to God as revealed in Jesus, the Christ, and man was promised the help of the Holy Spirit in overcoming self-centeredness and fear; the Greek hope for immortality was offered to all who would share in the death and resurrection of Jesus by joining the community of Christians and accepting baptism.

CHRISTIANITY'S CONTINUITY. Just as Christianity arose out of Judaism, so its continuity was rooted in that religion. The God of Judaism and the Old Testament scriptures, as well as the Jewish stress upon religion as involving all of life, have been central to Christianity throughout its history.

Dying and rising gods had been served for centuries in the ancient Near East. In Egypt, the cult of Isis and Osiris; in Palestine the ancient cult of Baal; and in Greece, the Dionysiac cult, proclaimed a god who had been put to death by his enemies, but rose again. Anyone who became a devotee of such a god was promised victory over death, which the god himself had already achieved. Christianity also proclaimed a dying and rising god, but with one important difference: that the man Jesus, who was put to death and resurrected, was not of mythological origin but had been an actual person. In the person of Jesus, Christianity possessed an element of continuity which made it impossible for any group to separate the Christian message from the historical Jesus, as the one hailed as the Jewish Messiah, or to vitiate Christianity by identifying a local savior god with Jesus. Or rather, whenever this is attempted, the Church has been able to correct the error.

Other elements of continuity in Christianity include the Bible, which combines the Jewish Old Testament with the New Testament as basic scripture, the Church as a universal fellowship, and the sacraments of baptism and of the Eucharist.

CHRISTIANITY'S ADAPTABILITY. In its ability to adapt to new geographical and cultural situations as it expands, Christianity has shown a remarkable viability. Its message is first to the individual, who is called to serve God as revealed in Christ. In the words of Paul (1 Cor. 7:17-24):

Let every one lead the life which the Lord has assigned to him, and in which God has called him. This is my rule in all the churches. Was any one at the time of his call already circumcised? Let him not seek to remove the marks of circumcision. Was any one at the time of his call uncircumcised? Let him not seek circumcision. For neither circumcision counts for anything nor uncircumcision, but keeping the commandments of God. Every one should remain in the state in which he was called. Were you a slave when called? Never mind. But if you can gain your freedom, avail yourself of the opportunity. For he who was called in the

Lord as a slave is a freedman of the Lord. Likewise he who was free when called is a slave of Christ. You were bought with a price; do not become slaves of men. So, brethren, in whatever state each was called, there let him remain with God.

Thus a Christian was called out of his society to become a slave of Christ, yet was to remain in it as a good citizen. His new relationship to God freed him from slavery to human appetites, such as self-indulgence in food or sex, and from fear of those in authority, as well as from contempt for social inferiors, hatred of enemies, and from the desire to dominate husband or wife. The Christian was called upon to enter a relationship with God which is described as being in God's kingdom. This new relationship was necessarily social, so that the person who began by seeking individual salvation found his attitudes and dealings with others immediately revolutionized.

Although the early Church did not oppose the system of slavery nor the tyranny of the Roman Empire, in the end it helped to abolish slavery and to change many aspects of life in the Roman Empire. The status of women and children was raised; sexual debauchery and other forms of licentiousness were attacked; in all sorts of ways Christianity helped to raise the level of personal and social living.

A discussion of the extent to which the Church has consistently followed this ideal, and how Christianity compares with its rivals, Buddhism and Islam, lies beyond our present scope. At this point we have been concerned only to describe the missionary dynamics which have helped to spread this religion to one-fourth of mankind.

CHRISTIANITY IN HISTORY

The initial expansion of Christianity was phenomenal in speed and extent. The movement spread primarily to the urban centers, and undoubtedly the most important factor in this spread was Diaspora Judaism, that is, Judaism outside Palestine. In most of the important cities of the Roman Empire, Judaism had established synagogues and was engaged in an active missionary program, proclaiming the god of Israel as the one true god, opposing the worship of idols, calling men to ethical living, and inviting them to become Jews. When the early Christians moved through the Roman world, proclaiming that the long-expected Jewish

Messiah had come in the person of Jesus, they went first to these Jewish centers and found a ready-made audience. We are told in the Book of Acts, again and again, that many Jews accepted faith in Christ and joined the Christian movement. The fact that Jewish missionary activity began to decline about this time lends support to the notion that much of the strength of Judaism was siphoned off into the Christian movement.

THE FIRST ONE HUNDRED YEARS. Soon after the death of Jesus (about 30 A.D.), the first Christian community in Jerusalem faced persecution from Jewish authorities, and some Christians were forced northward, where they founded new churches in Galilee and Syria. One persecutor, Saul of Tarsus, was converted to the new movement and joined other missionaries who had made Antioch in Syria their headquarters. He helped organize churches in Asia Minor and later founded churches in northern and southern Greece. Two main centers of his work were Ephesus and Corinth. Some of the letters he wrote in connection with his missionary activities constitute the earliest Christian literature.

Another early leader was Peter, a disciple of Jesus, in all likelihood the first to see the risen Lord. He was at first a leader of the church in Jerusalem, but later moved to Rome. Both Peter and Paul were executed by order of the Emperor Nero during the latter part of his reign (54-68).

In 66 A.D. a Jewish revolt against Rome broke out in Palestine and in the year 70 the Romans sacked Jerusalem and destroyed the Temple. Thereafter, Judaism turned more and more to Rabbinic legalism, and Christianity became increasingly independent of Judaism. Although Judaism was recognized as a legal religion under Roman rule and Jews were exempt from the requirement to worship the emperor, Christianity did not receive this exemption. Therefore, when Christians refused to accord divinity to the emperor, they faced persecution. Such New Testament writings as 1 Peter, Hebrews, and Revelation reflect the persecutions of the last quarter of the first century. The first serious persecution probably occurred toward the end of the reign of the Emperor Domitian (81-96). By 150 A.D., the Church had spread through the Roman world and the writings which later were to compose the New Testament were completed. With the relaxation of persecution, and with the realization that there might be an indefinite delay for the Parousia, the second coming of Jesus, to consummate the kingdom of God, the Church turned its attention to theological discussion and problems of ecclesiastical organization.

THE NEXT THOUSAND YEARS (150-1204 A.D.). Several important developments deserve brief mention. Creeds answered the need to define a Christian by some external test. In the context of persecution, it is necessary to have certain requirements for church membership. Otherwise, if someone were not serious about his faith, upon arrest he might betray his fellow Christians. If, in the name of love and tolerance, anybody could attend a Christian meeting, everyone was endangered. Also there were many who attempted to change the Christian message, or to identify it with one or another of the gnostic and mystery cults of the day, as did Marcion (c. 140 A.D.), the first heretic. To paraphrase Paul, if salvation is possible by Jewish law or by any mystery religion, then Christ and all the martyrs from Stephen, Paul, and Peter on must have died in vain. Thus creeds arose to define the content of Christian faith and to serve as tests for membership in the Church.

Since the attempt to define orthodoxy by requiring agreement with formal creeds is peculiar to biblical religions, and is especially characteristic of Christianity, we shall cite an example. The only creed which has been acceptable to both the Eastern and Western Churches, with minor alterations by various communions, is that stemming from the Council of Nicea (325 A.D.). The English translation, as it appears in *The Book of Common Prayer* of the Church of England, reads:

I believe in one God the Father Almighty, Maker of heaven and earth, And of all things visible and invisible:

And in one Lord Jesus Christ, the only-begotten Son of God; Begotten of his Father before all worlds, God of God, Light of Light, Very God of very God; Begotten, not made; Being of one substance with the Father; By whom all things were made. Who for us men and for our salvation came down from heaven, And was incarnate by the Holy Ghost of the Virgin Mary, And was made man. And was crucified also for us under Pontius Pilate; He suffered and was buried. And the third day he arose again according to the Scriptures. And ascended into heaven, And sitteth on the right hand of the Father: And he shall come again, with glory, to judge both the quick and the dead; Whose kingdom shall have no end.

And I believe in the Holy Ghost, The Lord, and Giver of life, Who proceedeth from the Father and the Son; Who with the Father and the Son together is worshipped and glorified; Who spake by the Prophets: And I believe one Catholic and Apostolic Church: I acknowledge one Baptism for the remission of sins. And I look for the Resurrection of the dead. And the life of the world to come. Amen.

In the fourth century, the Emperor Constantine (324-337) decreed that Christianity was an official religion of the empire. He presided, in 325 A.D., over the important Council of Nicea although he was not baptized until on his deathbed. Because of the pressures of barbarians from the north, he moved his capital from Rome to Byzantium, which was renamed Constantinople. By this time each important city had its own elected church head called *bishop*. The Bishop of Rome had assumed more and more importance, and when the capital was moved, he attempted, unsuccessfully, to dominate the Bishop of Constantinople.

In the middle of the seventh century Islam burst out of Arabia and made rapid inroads upon Christian territory. The Muslims swallowed up the Middle East, except for Asia Minor, swept across North Africa, and moved into Spain. By the eleventh century, even Asia Minor had succumbed and Constantinople was threatened.

THE EASTERN CHURCH. In 1054 occurred the Great Schism between the Church of Rome and the Eastern, or Greek, Church with its center in Constantinople. The Eastern Church has always followed the Patriarchal system wherein each area recognizes its own Metropolitan leader or Patriarch, and the Eastern group refused to accept the authority of the Bishop of Rome, now called the Pope or Holy Father. At different times leaders on each side attempted to heal the breach, but a reconciliation between the two major factions was doomed when the soldiers of the Fourth Crusade turned aside from their march against the Muslims and sacked Constantinople on Good Friday of the year 1204.

Although we have noted that the Eastern Church accepts the Nicene Creed (with the specific exception of the *filioque* clause, for they deny that the Holy Ghost proceeds from the Son) and is rooted in early Christianity as is the Church of Rome, through the centuries the Greek Church has developed its own emphases. Some of the more significant are:

Clergy and sacraments. The priesthood is allowed to marry, although a candidate for the office of bishop must be unmarried. The distinction between the clergy and the laity is not so radical as in the Roman and Protestant communions, and there is much wider participation by the laity in missionary and educational work. There are seven main sacraments, but these differ from those of the West at several points: infant baptism is practiced by triple immersion; the infant is confirmed or chrismated (anointed with oil) after baptism; leavened bread is used in the Eucharist; the sick are anointed as a means of grace for their recovery.

Emphasis upon community. There is neither a central authority for faith and practice such as the Papal rule of Rome, nor the stress upon the Bible and individual conscience as in Protestantism. Instead the emphasis is upon agreement on matters of doctrine and practice by the community of believers. In theology this finds expression in a sacramental view of life in which the material and spiritual worlds are considered equally sacred. Thus there is less stress than in the West upon sin, and on the body as evil, and also less asceticism. In worship this unity between the physical and spiritual worlds is given dramatic expression in the widespread use of ikons (painted pictures) of the Virgin Mary, Jesus, the Apostles and the saints. By this practice the feeling of communion between the worshipers and the ranks of the triumphant departed is realized.

THE EASTERN CHURCH IN HISTORY. In 1453 the Muslims finally conquered Constantinople and brought an end to the Byzantine Empire, and the center of ecclesiastical power shifted to Moscow. Under Islam the different patriarchates were tolerated, but further spread of Christianity was proscribed, and the Christians tended to become closeknit minorities with strong nationalistic leanings. This accounts in part for their more purely spiritual interpretation of Christianity with minimal concern for political and social problems. But the most significant result of Muslim domination was the stress on conserving the life of the Church in the midst of a hostile world, even though this meant a degree of stagnation.

The explorations of the Europeans in the sixteenth century reopened communications between Western Christendom and the national churches of Asia and Africa, and the Eastern Church began to stir with new vigor. A serious setback occurred in 1700 when Peter the Great (1682-1725), brought the Patriarchate of Moscow under the control of the

Russian state by establishing the Holy Governing Synod which he appointed to rule the Russian Church. This effectively silenced the Church as a political factor in Russia, and although the Russian Christians looked constantly for a leader to free the Church from state control, in the words of Nicolas Zernov, "no call to organized opposition was sounded and as a result, for more than two hundred years, the Russian Church lost the right to speak freely on any major moral or religious issue." (*Eastern Christendom: A Study of the Origin and Development of the Eastern Orthodox Church,* New York: G. P. Putnam's Sons, 1961, p. 158.)

In 1917 the Bolshevik revolution brought further persecutions and proscriptions to the beleaguered Russian Church, although one positive result of this attack was the emigration of Russian intellectuals to the urban centers of Western Europe and the Americas. They introduced many in the West to the theology and traditions of the Eastern Church. In 1943 the Soviet government found it strategic to the war effort to recognize the Church, since it had become clear that millions of Russians were still loyal to the faith. Although this recognition is at present little more than toleration, and is hedged with many restrictions, it is a significant factor in the increasing influence of the Eastern Church in world affairs.

In 1962, at the Third Assembly of the World Council of Churches (primarily till then a western Protestant body) in New Delhi, the Orthodox Churches of Russia, Romania, Bulgaria and Poland joined this ecumenical group. Although the Eastern Church has been less active in missionary work than has Protestantism, its close ties with Christianity in Asia and Africa should prove a tremendous asset to the Christian missionary movement in the coming decades.

THE WESTERN MEDIEVAL CHURCH. During the Dark Ages, after the barbarian tribes from Northern Europe and Western Asia eclipsed the civilization of Rome, the Church in Europe remained the main vehicle of Western education and culture. Monasteries were established where education was continued, and books preserved and copied, while the outside world underwent an age of illiteracy. Monastic culture also profited from the intellectual commerce between Christian and Muslim, for their relations were not restricted to armed conflict. Christian scholars rediscovered Plato and Aristotle in the Arabic translations of Muslim scholars. This in turn helped to make possible the contribution of such thinkers as Peter Abelard (1079-1142) and Thomas Aquinas (1226-74), who developed Christian theology to a remarkable level.

THE PROTESTANT REFORMATION. Through the centuries, the initial preaching and teaching of the Christian message of salvation was gradually altered, with more and more emphasis upon the sacraments as channels of the Holy Spirit. These seven sacraments were baptism, confirmation, the Eucharist, penance, holy orders, matrimony, and extreme unction. A self-perpetuating priesthood which received its authority from the Pope in Rome also had developed. In order for the sacraments to mediate God's power, it was necessary that they be administered by a priest. As a result, the Pope and the priestly hierarchy had vested in themselves tremendous coercive power. If an individual went against the authority of the Church, he could be deprived of salvation and the hope of immortality, by means of excommunication from the fellowship and sacraments of the Church. If a ruler disobeyed the Church, or if the Church wanted to influence his actions, a whole nation could be placed under the papal ban. This meant that no priest in that country could administer any sacraments. When the people were deprived of baptism, the Eucharist, extreme unction, and even marriage, they usually forced the ruler to accept the dictates of the Church.

Many factors contributed to the violent break with Rome which culminated in the work of Martin Luther (1483-1546). His challenge to the Church in 1517 was not the first protest; these had been going on for several centuries; they included such noteworthy occurrences as the Waldensian movement in Italy in the twelfth century and the revolt of John Hus in Bohemia in the fifteenth. Feudalism was breaking up, the universities were growing in influence, and national states claiming new loyalties were forming. Luther's position is typical of basic Protestant thought and represents the reformed message of salvation which opposed that of Rome.

Luther was a priest and a professor of biblical study at the University of Wittenberg. He claimed to preach a return to biblical doctrine. Much of the strength of his movement was made possible by the invention of printing and the translations of the Bible into the vernaculars. His teaching was, essentially, threefold:

(1) Man is saved by faith alone (*sola fide*); it is God's power and

spirit which justify man, not the sacraments of the Church nor the ritual acts of the priest.

(2) The Bible, not the teachings of the Church Fathers nor the authority of the Pope, is the sole source of true doctrine and the sole guide to Christian conduct (*sola scriptura*).

(3) The "priesthood of all true believers" makes each man directly responsible to God; ecclesiastical authority does not have the power to save or condemn.

The result of this rising tide of Protestant criticism of the Roman Church was a new and vigorous branch of Christendom which now claims much of Northern Europe and is strong in North America. At the same time, the Counter Reformation in the Roman Church produced many important changes often overlooked by the average Protestant. Moreover, the tendency of Protestantism to split up into subsects over such minutiae as forms of baptism or details of church government is a problem of growing magnitude, especially to the young churches of Africa and Asia.

THE MODERN PERIOD. The eighteenth century Enlightenment, with its stress upon reason and science, made heavy inroads into Christianity, especially in Europe, and the United States. In the nineteenth century, the writings of Darwin, Marx, and Freud presented a serious challenge to Christian thought. In Protestantism this challenge was met by leading theologians with the scholarly discipline of biblical criticism and the fearless re-evaluation of Christian dogmas. In Roman Catholic circles, accommodation has been much slower, but there has been a constant movement in the direction of reinterpreting the teachings of the Church to fit the findings of science and reason.

Two important developments should be noted here. The first is the tremendous missionary enterprise of the entire Western Church that has carried Christian teachings to the far corners of the earth. The other is the disturbing fact that it is primarily the "Christian" nations of Europe and North America who have fought two World Wars in this century. The positive gain of that missionary enterprise, which poured human sacrifices in untold numbers and vast sums of money into the work of spreading the Gospel and building schools and hospitals for the peoples of Asia and Africa, is offset by the colonial policies of the very countries sending the missionaries. Since mainly the Caucasian countries have sent missionaries to colored races, Christianity has come to be identified as the "white man's religion." In the present competition with the other two missionary religions, Buddhism and Islam, the fact that the latter two are found mainly among colored peoples gives them a potent appeal.

Chapter Seven

ISLAM

Islam is the correct name for the religion often called *Mohammedanism*, which arose in the seventh century A.D. under the leadership of Mohammed. Islam means *submission* to the will of Allah, the God of Mohammed. The members of this religion call themselves *Muslims*, "those who submit." Islam, the youngest of the biblical religions, arose in the context of Judaism and Christianity and reflects much of the theology and eschatology of Zoroastrianism. To the Muslim the Jewish and Christian scriptures and the Old Testament prophets and Jesus were all channels for Allah's revelations prior to the final revelation of the true religion, Islam.

Mohammed and the Rise of Islam

THE ARABIAN WORLD IN MOHAMMED'S TIME. The Arabian Peninsula consists of about one million square miles, much of which is desert; even the more hospitable sections are semiarid. Mohammed lived in Mecca, which lies near the southwest coast of the peninsula. In the seventh century, this region was still only half-civilized and most of the inhabitants lived much as in the days of Abraham, twenty-five centuries earlier. There was no unified government in the peninsula and tribal confederations held power in different areas; such peace as existed was merely an armed truce. Colonies of Jews and Christians lived in Mecca and nearby communities, but the usual religion was a fairly primitive polytheism.

THE LIFE OF MOHAMMED. Mohammed was born in Mecca in 570 A.D., shortly after the death of his father, who had been a member of the powerful Quraish tribe. After Mohammed's mother died when he was six, his grandfather cared for him briefly, then his father's brother, Abu Talib, brought him up. As a young man, Mohammed traveled with caravans as far as Syria, and according to one tradition, even to Egypt. When he was twenty-five he married a wealthy widow, Khadijah, who was in the caravan trade. Their marriage was a happy one, although the sons born to them died, and of four daughters only one, Fatima, lived to maturity.

When he was about forty, in 610 A.D., Mohammed began to have a series of disturbing visions. His secure economic status after his marriage had made possible periods of meditation and solitude. He spent some time in a cave near Mecca and there one day the angel Gabriel appeared to him. Mohammed reported that the angel commanded him:

> Recite, in the name of thy Lord who has created,
> Created man from clots of blood.
> Recite, seeing that thy Lord is the most generous,
> Who has taught by the pen,
> Taught man what he did not know.*

The word translated "recite" is the word which gives its title to the Koran (Arabic, *Qur'ān*), and means the reciting, or reading.

This first vision was soon followed by many others; when Mohammed reported them to Khadijah, she encouraged him to be led by his revelations. He began to proclaim that Allah is the one true deity, and that no other god might be served. He also announced that it was Allah's message to mankind which had been revealed to him in the series of visions, and that he had been appointed by Allah to be his messenger to the world.

Mohammed's proclamation aroused immediate opposition because it constituted an attack on the tribal religions of the Arabs. He had denounced the local gods as false, and worship of them as idolatrous. Fortunately, both Khadijah, and Mohammed's uncle, Abu Talib, had prestige and influence and were able to protect Mohammed against attack. He had few converts at first, however, and opposition grew stronger, so that some of the prophet's followers fled to Abyssinia and established a Muslim community there. The deaths of both Khadijah and Abu Talib in 620 endangered the Meccan Muslims by depriving them of the tribal support which these relatives of their leader had guaranteed.

The nearby city of Yathrib, to the northeast, welcomed some of Mo-

---

* *Qur'an*, Sura XCVI:1-5, Arthur Jeffery, trans. *Islam: Muhammad and His Religion* (New York: The Liberal Arts Press, Inc. The Library of Religion, LLA 137, 1958), p. 4, used by permission of The Bobbs-Merrill Company, Inc.

hammed's followers and soon others went to the new community which was established there. Finally a plot was organized against the life of Mohammed and on July 16, 622 A.D., he fled to Yathrib with his close companions. This flight, called *hegira,* or *hijra,* marks the beginning of Islam as a religion. All Muslim dates are calculated from this day and designated A.H., meaning "in the year of the Hijra." Since the lunar calendar used by the Arabs gains an extra year every thirty-three solar years, a table of conversion dates is required to relate Muslim and Christian dates. Yathrib, the city which offered refuge to the prophet, was renamed Medina, which is the Arabic word for city, meaning the "City of the Prophet."

In Medina Mohammed became both the political and the religious leader. With the rapid expansion of the community, however, economic needs, especially food, soon became pressing. Permission was granted to attack caravans in the name of the new religion; since most of the booty, according to the prophet's decree, could be kept by the fighters, it is not surprising that many new converts joined the movement. Then a strong force came out of Mecca eager to defeat and scatter Mohammed's followers, who had now become a menace. Against what appeared to be insuperable odds, the Muslims won a decisive victory, and the fortunes of the community dramatically changed. At the same time, however, the Jews and Christians, who up to this time had been sympathetic to Mohammed's cause, now began to oppose him. But the new movement no longer needed their support. After some years of war with various tribes, the Muslims were able to return to Mecca, victorious. Whereas at first Mohammed had taught that Allah desired his followers to pray facing Jerusalem, he now changed the direction of prayer to Mecca, and also made the ancient shrine in Mecca, the Ka'ba, a center for religious pilgrimage.

By the time of his death, Mohammed had received pledges of loyalty from all over Arabia and his movement was expanding at an increasing rate. In 732 he died of a fever brought on by old war wounds. At his death, the first *Caliph* ("successor"), Abu Bekr, was chosen as leader of the Muslim community; under him the religion continued its amazing expansion.

THE SCRIPTURES OF ISLAM. Mohammed was familiar with the traditions of both Judaism and Christianity. One of the Five Doctrines of Islam is that Allah revealed his partial will from time to time in the past, but he finally completed his revelation through Mohammed in the *Quran* (Koran).

According to Muslim tradition, the Quran contains only the words of Mohammed when, in a prophetic trance, he served as Allah's spokesman. It is composed of 114 *suras,* chapters, which have been arranged approximately by length, the longer suras coming first and the shorter ones toward the end. Many of the suras were written down during Mohammed's lifetime; the rest were put together from memory after his death. The contents are jumbled and, since the style is poetic, many allusions are obscure. Muslim doctrine is that the Quran is an exact copy of the original in heaven; therefore no translation can substitute for the original Arabic. It is referred to by such titles as the Glorious Quran and the Mighty Quran.

Although the Quran represents Allah's complete revelation to Mohammed, many teachings, rulings, and sayings of the prophet also were preserved by the Muslim community. Since Islam expanded rapidly, many situations arose for which the Quran contained no explicit instructions. Accordingly, nonquranic sayings were compiled over the years and finally were codified in the *Hadith* ("tradition"). The actual text of a saying preserving a Hadith or tradition is called a *sunna* ("custom") meaning that this was Mohammed's way (custom) of acting or thinking.

THE MESSAGE OF MOHAMMED. The teachings of Mohammed have been preserved with more accuracy than those of the founder of any other religion; a description of the prophet's message and world view is essentially a summary of orthodox Muslim thought. Although Muslim theology was developed to a high degree by the Doctors of the Law, the *Ulama* (learned ones), especially in the Near East, North Africa, and Southern Europe, the basic beliefs and practices of orthodox Muslims throughout the world of Islam, from Morocco to the Philippine Islands, are contained in the "Five Doctrines" and the "Five Pillars of the Faith." These are all mentioned in the Quran, although there is some slight modification in detail, and more in interpretation, in later Islamic thought.

THE FIVE DOCTRINES OF ISLAM. There are five beliefs to which a Muslim must subscribe. A sixth, which is not mandatory, is often added.

(1) There is only one true god, Allah. The name *Allah* is known to have been the name of a deity before the time of Mohammed. As with names in general, its derivation is uncertain; one suggested derivation is *al illah,* meaning *the god.*

Allah has seven characteristics, although his ultimate being cannot be fathomed by human reason. He has absolute unity, and is all-seeing, all-hearing, all-speaking, all-knowing, all-willing and all-powerful. He has more authority specifically ascribed to him than any other deity in the world's religions.

(2) There are angels, chief of whom is Gabriel; he first appeared to Mohammed to reveal to him that he had been called by Allah. Islam also believes in a fallen angel called Iblis (the Greek *diabolos*), also called Shaitan (the Hebrew Satan); as well as in the minions of Shaitan, the djinn (demons).

(3) There are, as we have said, four inspired books: the Torah of Moses, the Zabur (Psalms) of David, the Injil (Evangel) of Jesus, and the Quran. The Quran is Allah's final message, addressed to all mankind, not merely to Jew and Christian. The Quran supersedes all previous revelation and abrogates any conflicting claims to truth. Yet Jews, Christians, and Zoroastrians, since each belongs to the community of a "people of a book," are to be treated with more tolerance than pagans, since they are the custodians of part of Allah's revelation.

(4) There are twenty-eight prophets of Allah, including Mohammed. Most of them are well-known biblical persons and include Adam, Noah, Abraham, Moses, David, Jonah, Jesus, and John. But the last and greatest of the prophets, and the "seal" of prophecy, is Mohammed, messenger of Allah to all the world.

(5) There will be a "last day." The eschatological teachings of the Quran are vivid and dramatic, and have assumed great importance in Muslim theology. A Muslim must believe in the resurrection of the body, in a final judgment, and a final destiny in heaven or hell, depending upon Allah's decision. Heaven is a man's paradise (women are shown small consideration) and is pictured in most appealing terms. Hell and its torments are described even more vividly; Hell is the abode of those who oppose the teachings of Mohammed and the will of Allah.

(6) A sixth doctrine *Kismet* ("fate") is taught, but need not be accepted by the faithful. This asserts that all that happens is foreor-

dained. This is interpreted fatalistically by many, but the higher interpretation of this doctrine affirms only that everything in creation is completely under the control of Allah, even those happenings of which
Allah does not approve.

THE FIVE PILLARS OF THE FAITH. Just as there are five
doctrines which must be accepted, there are five duties which must be
performed and which support the faith of the community. To these, also,
is added a sixth pillar, which is not mandatory. The duties are:

First, to recite the *Shahadah,* also kown as the *Kalima* (word):
"There is no god but Allah and Mohammed is the Prophet of Allah."
This confession that one is a Muslim must be stated publicly and with
conviction to make one a believer.

Second, to perform *salat,* or prayers, five times daily. This consists of the recitation of stated prayers and a series of postures and genu-
flections while facing the holy city, Mecca. To face Mecca is termed
qibla, and the direction is indicated in a mosque by the *mihrab,* a
depression in the appropriate wall. The Quran prescribes only three
daily prayers, but early Hadith changed this to five, to be said at dawn,
noon, afternoon, evening, and night. Muslims are summoned to prayer
by the call of the Muezzin (Arabic, *mu'adhdhin*) who stands in the
minaret (lighthouse, *cf.* Hebrew *menorah*) to announce the times for
prayer.

Third, to give alms, *zakat,* to the Muslim community. Zakat
means "righteousness"; at first it required that a Muslim offer a portion
of his income-producing property, but later this tended to be calculated
as one-fortieth of his income. It must be a voluntary offering, given to
help widows, orphans, the sick, and all others who are unfortunate. In
performing this duty, the fact is stressed that one is sharing out of the
abundance which Allah gave.

Fourth, to fast during the month of Ramadan, the ninth month
of the Muslim lunar year. There are other periods and types of fasting,
but this is the most dramatic, and is observed by most of the people, much
as Christian Lent is observed in Catholic countries. During the daylight
hours the Muslim must not swallow even his spittle, and must abstain
from sexual enjoyment. The night is not mentioned, so the faithful eat
and drink at night, and the less orthodox even indulge themselves after
dusk. Since the Muslim calendar of twelve lunar months regresses
through the solar year, once every thirty-three years, when Ramadan

occurs in summer, Muslims in hot, dry countries, for instance, find the fast extremely demanding.

Fifth, the *Hajj,* the official pilgrimage to Mecca in the twelfth month, to be performed at least once during a Muslim's life. The pilgrimage is costly and dangerous, and after reaching Mecca, great physical endurance is required for participation in all aspects of the rite. Consequently, one is required to make the pilgrimage only if he is free, a Muslim, of age, and physically and mentally able. One is allowed to have another person make the Hajj for him as proxy, and many pilgrims meet the expenses of the journey by receiving help from those who cannot go. Over the centuries, the Hajj has served as an important unifying force for Islam.

A sixth pillar, which is not mandatory, is *Jihad,* the Holy War. Of course this is meant to imply only a war in defense of Islam, although it has also been used to support aggression. In the First World War, the Central Powers attempted to institute a Jihad against the Allies, without success; more recently there has been some talk of attempting a Jihad against the State of Israel. In all probability, the national interests of Muslim countries will make a true Jihad increasingly unlikely.

THE ISLAMIC WORLD VIEW. Although the basic features of Muslim belief are included in the doctrine and practice, a brief summary of the seven items in our scheme follows.

The cosmos. The universe is the creation of Allah and is conceived in the three-level form of biblical thought. Mankind lives on earth; Allah resides in a heaven above the earth; and Shaitan and his minions in a hell beneath the earth. As the world is created, so will it some day be judged, and all mortal beings will enter either heaven or hell.

Deity. Islam proclaims a strict monotheism, with Allah as the sole deity. No worship of any other being is permitted, and no gods are to be associated with Allah. He has no partners or equals, nor can he have a son, as in Christianity. The entire universe, including even Shaitan and his djinns, is completely under Allah's authority. Islamic thought lays continual stress upon the omnipotence of Allah and the complete dependence of all creation upon his pleasure.

Man. Man as a created being is composed of a body and a soul. As a creature, his purpose in life is to obey and serve Allah by complete submission to his will. Women are created a degree below men and are to be obedient to their husbands, who are to treat them with kindness.

Man's plight. Mohammed's message emphasized that in some way mankind had lost its way and turned from worship and the service of Allah. As long as man follows his own mistaken ways, or worships false gods, his life will be without meaning or purpose. But in this world evil can overtake even the faithful. This is true partly because Allah permits Shaitan and his djinns a measure of freedom in this world. Even the Muslim who is faithful may experience misery and disaster if Allah, in his infinite but inscrutable wisdom, desires or allows this to happen. But the greatest cause of misery for man is the stubborn refusal of infidels to submit to the will of Allah.

Salvation. Just as Islam means submission, and a Muslim is one who submits to the will of Allah, true salvation is to be found in complete surrender to Allah. In addition one is to follow Allah's will as revealed in the Quran through his messenger, Mohammed. Acceptance of the five doctrines and faithful performance of the five pillars are also requisite to obtaining the fullest and most meaningful life. But Allah, whose character it is to be compassionate and merciful, alone can save or destroy. Therefore submission to Allah is reasonable, since he is the author of all true salvation.

Conduct. The Quran contains all that is necessary to live a holy life. Several specific teachings deserve mention, however, as distinctive to Muslim practice. Eating swine's flesh is forbidden, reflecting the influence of Judaism. Although not enjoined in the Quran, circumcision is practiced and is traced back to Abraham and his son Ishmael, who are claimed as the ancestors of the Arabs. Gambling and drinking alcohol are forbidden, perhaps reflecting the early growth of Islam in army camps where such practices can be divisive. Usury is condemned and generosity commended. Family life is given high praise, but the quranic teaching that women are inferior to men has tended to make them slaves to their husbands' desires. The ruling that a man is allowed up to four wives should be understood, however, not in terms of the Western ideal of monogamy, but in terms of the cultural background of Islam. Mohammed claimed that extra marriages were for the benefit of the wives. Thus, in the warfare of early Islam many of Mohammed's close friends were killed, leaving widows whom he married to insure their security. In addition, the inheritance laws of the Quran are very specific in protecting the rights of widows and orphans, as well as the rights of a wife who is mistreated by her husband.

Destiny. What is to happen to men after death, and to Allah's creation at the end of this age, is included in the fifth doctrine concerning the last day. The eschatology of Islam, however, has a most important relationship to faith and practice. Since one has but this single life in which to decide for or against Allah, and since where one is to spend eternity is determined by Allah, the fear of hell and the hope of heaven serve as potent sanctions for daily ethical living.

ISLAM AS A MISSIONARY RELIGION

Islam experienced the most dramatic expansion of any religion when it broke out of the Arabian Peninsula in the seventh century and spread north, west, and east. Like an avalanche its totalitarianism swallowed everything in its path and supplanted with Islam the religious and cultural patterns of the areas it invaded. Today this religion is the dominant faith in a belt of countries which extends across the world eastward from Gibraltar to the Philippine Islands, and its followers number over four hundred millions, or about one-seventh of mankind. Islam has all the attributes of a missionary religion—a universal message, a peerless continuity, and a good measure of adaptability.

THE UNIVERSALISM OF ISLAM. The religion proclaimed by Mohammed is simplicity itself. One has only to accept Mohammed's claim that he was the true and final prophet of Allah and to submit to the will of Allah as revealed in the Quran. Allah is beneficent and merciful and is eager to accept the submission of all. There is no distinction of color or race; neither social class nor condition of servitude is a deterrent to becoming a Muslim. The only limitation on the universality of Islam's message is the teaching that women are inferior to men, but until this century this apparently has not been a significant factor. No esoteric knowledge is required which only the few can achieve, no difficult asceticism calls upon one to forsake the world. Anyone can enter the Muslim community and become a full member at any time and in any place.

THE CONTINUITY OF ISLAM. The continuity of Islam is monolithic, being simply an extension of the five doctrines and the five pillars of the faith. The Jewish and Christian scriptures, and the folk traditions of Arabia which trace the ancestry of the Arabs back to Abraham, gave Mohammed roots for his new revelation. The loyalty of all

Muslims to the prophet, to Allah, the Quran and Hadith, and the beliefs and practices of the community have maintained Islam with little change for over thirteen centuries.

THE ADAPTABILITY OF ISLAM. It is on the score of adaptability that Islam has experienced difficulties. And it is likely that it will have increasing problems, as it seeks to adapt to Western science, technology, and political and social innovations. Mohammed's message was first proclaimed in Mecca which, though an urban community, was set in the vast expanse of semiarid land of Arabia Felix, and the Quran's teachings fit a fairly unsophisticated culture. Although scholars protest that Islam cannot be explained in terms of its desert background; nevertheless it is true that, throughout Muslim history, it has been difficult to relate the Quran to the many new situations which the Muslims met in their conquests. Islam, for instance, very soon overran much of the Byzantine empire in Asia Minor but rejected much of its culture, including its more speculative Greek ways of thought. In fact, Islam has tended to be restricted to the broad belt of semitropical countries from Morocco to the Philippines. Islam has not followed the pattern of Judaism which, under Christian pressures, formed its own closed communities within which it practiced Sabbath observance, kosher food laws, and intermarriage. Instead Islam, during most of its history, either has completely dominated the political, economic, and social life of an area or has tended to withdraw.

THE EXPANSION OF ISLAM

In the seventh century when Islam set out to dominate the world, two powers held sway in Mediterranean lands and in western Asia: the Greek empire of Byzantium and the Sassanian dynasty of Persia. Both were overthrown, and with little resistance, the Muslims marched to Spain in the west and into northwest India on the east. Christians, Jews, and Zoroastrians were treated fairly tolerantly and were not forced into conversion. Gradually in some places, more rapidly in others, Islam became not only the dominant political power but the religion of the majority as well. Although Constantinople, the capital of the Byzantine empire, did not fall to Islam until 1453, most Byzantine territories were swallowed up in Islam, and Christianity lost many to the new faith.

in part because of Islam's vigorous appeal, but also because of Christianity's own internal dissensions.

To the east, Persia gradually became almost entirely Muslim, but in India, after initial success in what is now Afghanistan and Pakistan, the advance bogged down. By the twelfth century, Islam had made further gains in India, but never penetrated to any depth south of the Vindhya divide. As a result of the missionary activities of traders and settlers, China today is estimated to have about thirty million Muslims, mostly in west China. As early as the seventh century, Muslim traders had carried Islam to Indonesia, but it was not until the fourteenth century that a positive program of expansion began. Today Indonesia is an important Muslim country, numbering over ninety million Muslims. In the fifteenth and sixteenth centuries, Islam moved into the southeast Pacific and converted many of the inhabitants of Borneo and the Philippines, arriving just a few decades before Spanish Christian missionaries. Christian conversions, therefore, have tended to be limited in this whole area.

In the nineteenth century, when the slave trade was abolished (at least legally) in Africa, there was a surge of conversions of natives of East and West Africa. The Muslims, who were active in the slave trade, had not sought to spread Islam in these areas since they are not permitted to enslave fellow Muslims. Today Islam is carrying on an intensive missionary program, much of it in competition with Christian missions. Most important in the present-day expansion of Islam, however, is the fact that Muslim countries average the highest birth rate in the world, further encouraged by the practice of polygyny.

THE STRUCTURE OF ISLAM

There is no real counterpart to the Christian church in Islam (although all Muslims count themselves part of the *Ummah,* or community of the faithful), nor is there a priesthood or holy orders. The structure is much closer to that of Judaism, in that men trained in Muslim law guide the affairs of the community. Although Islam has been held together primarily by its teaching and practice, every Muslim is under the authority directly or indirectly of various religious leaders.

THE CALIPHATE. Caliph means "successor" and refers to the line of leaders who inherited the authority of Mohammed as head of the community. The first caliph, Abu Bekr—a comrade-in-arms of the prophet—was succeeded in turn by Omar and Othman; the fourth caliph was Ali, Mohammed's cousin and also his son-in-law, since he married Fatima. Ali was assassinated before he really gained political control. After him, the caliphate fell into the hands of a dynasty known as the *Ummayyad,* soon to be replaced by the Abbasid caliphs. The latter continued in power until the thirteenth century, when the Sultan of Turkey made the caliphate synonymous with his rule. In 1922, when Turkey became a republic, the caliphate was abolished.

THE FOUR SCHOOLS OF LAW. Fairly early in Muslim history, four main schools of law or interpretation of the Quran and Hadith arose. These are the Hanifite, which extends orthodox teaching by analogy; the Malakite, which depends upon consensus of the community; the Shafiite, which opposed the Hanifite school by stressing a return to the Quran; and the Hanbalite, which like the Shafiite, is conservative in its interpretation.

Each national and geographic area tends to be dominated by one of these schools, and every Muslim is expected to live by one of the main schools of interpretation and to follow the guidance and authority of the *Ulamas,* those learned in the law. The Ulamas collectively represent various levels of religious leadership and have been the main preservers of doctrine and tradition.

THE TWO MAIN SECTS. There are two main sectarian movements in Islam, the Sunnis and the Shiites. The Sunnis follow the tradition of the followers of Mohammed (contained in the Hadith) and are the dominant group. The Shiites are partisans of Ali who claim that Ali was the legitimate successor to Mohammed. They are especially prominent in Persia and India. In the ninth century, a subsect, the Ismailis, arose out of the Shiites. They teach that there is always an Imam, or leader, directly representing Allah on earth. This group is headed by the Aga Khan.

THE TWO ORDERS. Although orthodox Muslim thought is inimical to mysticism, stressing instead the transcendence of Allah, an important order of mystics, the Sufis, has had great influence. The term *sufi,* from the word for wool, refers to the rough wool robes worn by mendicants who have renounced the world. They undoubtedly were influenced in their theology and religious expression by Christian mystics, and also by Hindu, Mahayana Buddhist, and other monistic thinkers of the areas bordering on Persia. They also reflect the universal tendency of religious movements to interpret religious experience in terms of the immanence of the world of the spirit.

The other order is that of the Wahhabi, which places great importance upon the transcendence of Allah. It is puritanical in practice and fanatically orthodox. The movement arose in the seventeenth century in Arabia. The Wahhabi not only have gained control of the holy city of Mecca, but also have great influence in the oil-producing regions of south Arabia. This conservative order represents primarily a reaction against the degeneration of Islam from within and the influence of Western ways from without. They are an important factor in political developments in the Near East.

Islam Today

Islam has been a significant force in the history of the West. The Christian Crusades against Islam were a testimony to the power and threat that the Muslims represented during our medieval period. Yet for the past several centuries Islam has been relatively quiescent. In this century, however, it appears to be undergoing, almost overnight, changes which Christianity experienced through several centuries. The breakup of the Ottoman empire at the end of the First World War led to the creation of several new Muslim countries, and with the abandonment of colonialism, either partially or completely, by European powers, many new Muslim states have joined the United Nations.

Probably the creation of new and separate Muslim states will tend to place nationalism ahead of Islam in the loyalties of the inhabitants of those states. Western notions of democracy and of the equality of women are causing ferment and present a relentless challenge to orthodox ways. Western science and secular forces of every sort are also taking their toll. These influences are offset, at least partially, by modernization of religious teaching in some Muslim universities and by attempts to extend Muslim influence, e.g., Pakistan's effort to create a genuinely Muslim state. In this case, it appears difficult to have a constitution modeled after the British pattern and also to insist that the government be genuinely Muslim, conforming to quranic teaching.

There is increasing missionary activity, which also includes educational and other social programs. With Muslims representing both the colored races and the colonial peoples, Islam has an entrée in Africa and Asia which Christianity has found difficult to match. No doubt contemporary Islam is much healthier and more aggressive than it has been at any time in the past five hundred years.

Part Three

THE RELIGIONS OF INDIA

Chapter Eight

THE LAND OF INDIA

With our European heritage, we are accustomed to thinking of Palestine, Greece, and Rome as the sources of our religion and culture. The subcontinent of India has a significance for all of Asia which is even more basic to its classical heritage than the legacy of the Mediterranean countries to the West. India has been the mother of four of the world's living religions: Hinduism, Jainism, Buddhism, and the Sikh movement. One of these, Buddhism, has moved out into all Asia and today directly influences the thought and lives of the hundreds of millions who live in Burma, Thailand, China, Korea, Japan, and the other countries of Asia. In addition, the great Hindu epics, the *Mahabharata* and the *Ramayana,* have become part of the traditional art and literature of most of South Asia. The country which has contributed so much to the life of Asia has rightly been called "Mother India."

GEOGRAPHICAL CONSIDERATIONS. Although recent political events have led to the division of the Indian subcontinent into three new countries, Hindustan, Pakistan, and Ceylon, for our purposes the entire area of classical India may be considered as a unit. Two noteworthy geographical features are its subtropical climate and its relative isolation. It has often been suggested that the tendency to denial of the world or to escapism in India's thought may be traced to the enervatingly hot and humid climate of much of the country. Although she has experienced a series of invasions, India has had little record of conquest or expansion because of her geographical location: to the west the barriers of the Indian Ocean and the deserts of Baluchistan; to the northwest, the Hindu-Kush Mountains; to the north, the Himalayas; to the northeast, dense, tropical jungle; and to the east and south, again the ocean.

Most of India's invaders have entered her northwest border through the passes of the Hindu-Kush Mountains. Each successive wave has tended to push the members of the preceding invasion southward, and eventually to pack them in diverse layers from the southern tip to the north. At the same time, the geographical structure of the country has made travel between north and south somewhat difficult. The bulk of the population is concentrated in the great northern Gangetic plain. South of this plain lie the Vindhya hills which run east-west across the land and divide the south from the north. The main river valleys of central and south India also run east-west and further impede travel and communication. These factors all help to explain why the peoples, languages, and subcultures of India are so varied and why it is difficult to make accurate generalizations about the religious life of India.

THE PEOPLES OF INDIA. The three main divisions of the ethnic groups of India are the pre-Dravidians, the Dravidians, and the Indo-Europeans. The oldest stratum, the pre-Dravidians, are jungle and hill tribes scattered throughout central and south India, and represent a wide diversity in language and racial types. The Dravidians probably infiltrated India from the west and northwest before 3000 B.C. Today, the Dravidian group of languages is dominant in central and south India. They have not been linked to any Indo-European or Semitic language. Some of the major Dravidian languages are Tamil (under 25,000,000 speakers), Telugu (perhaps 30,000,000), and Malayalam (about 10,000,000). Each of these has an extensive literature.

The dominant ethnic group, however, in the culture and religion of India stems from the Indo-Aryan invaders of the second millennium B.C. They, as we said, entered in successive waves from the northwest, engulfing most of the Dravidian civilization of the Indus Valley and imposing their rule upon most of the country. It was long thought that the Aryans completely supplanted the earlier civilization, but with the archaeological discoveries since the 1920's of the prehistoric cities of

Mohenjo-daro and Harappa in the valley of the Indus, much evidence has been accumulating that pre-Aryan religion and philosophy exerted a strong influence upon the invaders and have continued to play an important role throughout Indian history.

The language spoken by the Aryans was a proto-Sanskrit, cognate with Persian, Greek, Latin, and the Slavonic and Teutonic language groups. The massive accumulation of Sanskrit literature of India, beginning with the famous Vedic writings, is in the tradition of the language of these early invaders. Today about three-fourths of the inhabitants of India speak a language with a Sanskrit base.

THE MAJOR RELIGIONS. Six main aspects of the religions of India are surveyed in this chapter. In the next chapter, Chapter Nine, three important periods of Hinduism will be described: the Vedic age; the classical age of the *Upanishads;* and the age of popular Hinduism and the *Bhakti* cults. Chapter Ten covers the heresy of Jainism which, unlike Buddhism, survives in the India of today. Chapter Eleven deals with Buddhism; Chapter Twelve, with the religion of the Sikhs.

BASIC INDIAN CONCEPTS. The religions which have arisen in India all have certain basic presuppositions in common, even though there are subtle, and very important, differences in the ways in which these axiomatic truths are regarded. Three of these presuppositions are of central importance and characterize Indian religion as opposed to the religions of the Near East, or those of China and Japan.

Samsara. Whereas biblical religions, for instance, assume a creator god who ordains but one life for each individual, Indian thought assumes that each person has lived several lives before his present one. The word *samsara* means "to move across," or "to wander," and is used to convey the concept of transmigration, of passing from one existence to another.

Karma. The word karma is cognate with our word *create* and refers to that which one does, one's personal thoughts and actions. In Indian religions what one does with the totality of his present life determines the nature of his rebirth. That is to say, the level of his birth as beast, insect or man, his good fortune or evil lot, are all determined by his previous lives and accumulated karma.

Nirvana. The ultimate goal of Indian religion is to stop the cycle of rebirths in which each person is caught. The word *nirvana* is made up of two elements, the negative *nir,* and the root *va,* meaning "to blow."

When a person dies, the fires of his body go out, become cool. So nirvana means going out, waning away, or loss of selfhood. The operational content of this word differs in Indian religions, but all agree that the goal of life is to cease to be reborn, to achieve nirvana; that is to obtain release (*moksha*) from samsara.

As we turn our attention to an analysis of the various Indian religions, these terms will serve as common denominators. Our study begins, however, with the early, Vedic period before the ideas of rebirth and escape arose.

Chapter Nine

HINDUISM

Hinduism has no founder. It has grown up in India and can be identified with the main stream of Indian culture. One cannot in a full sense be a convert to Hinduism, but must be born a Hindu, since one's status is determined primarily by birth. Thus, even though India's culture has influenced the whole of South and Southeast Asia, Hinduism has scarcely concerned itself with missionary work. This chapter traces the main developments of Hinduism chronologically, merely mentioning the heresies of Buddhism and Jainism and the religion of the Sikhs. These will be outlined in subsequent chapters.

RELIGION OF THE VEDIC AGE

PRE-ARYAN INDIA. It was only in 1921 that Sir John Marshall opened up the modern study of the Indus Valley civilization in northwest India. This culture predates Vedic religion. Two important sites have been excavated, Mohenjo-daro in Sind and Harappa, farther north in the central Punjab. This civilization flourished c. 3200-2500 B.C.; it is certain that there was some connection between this culture and that of Mesopotamia. The evidence for this consists primarily of finds of pottery and figurines which are parallel to those found in Mesoptamia; showing that in all likelihood one culture borrowed from the other.

The early inhabitants of India, just referred to, may have been the ancestors of the present-day Dravidians of southeast India. They had a pictographic script not yet deciphered; we therefore know almost nothing about their religious beliefs or practices, except as these are reconstructed by the projection of later thought onto such prehistoric material as we have. Nevertheless, it is becoming increasingly evident that much of the mainstream of Indian thought, represented by such major schools as the Samkhya philosophy, and reflected in Buddhism, Jainism, and the cult of Shiva, springs from this pre-Aryan civilization.

THE COMING OF THE ARYANS. This early Indus Valley

civilization was overrun and largely destroyed by a series of invasions from the northwest, beginning as early as the end of the third millennium B.C. The newcomers called themselves *Aryans,* a word which means "noble" or "aristocrat," and is cognate with the modern name for Persia, Iran; it was misused by the German Nazis who referred to themselves as Aryans. The language spoken by these invaders belonged to the Indo-European family and was the prototype of the later sacred language, Sanskrit. The major contemporary languages of northern India descend from this Aryan tongue.

SOURCES FOR THE STUDY OF VEDIC RELIGION. The historical beginnings of Hinduism go back to the invading Aryans, who brought with them religious practices and accompanying cultic hymns, prayers, and chants. By 1000 B.C., the hymns were held sacred and had become the nucleus of Vedic literature. The word *veda* is cognate with the English word "wise," the German *wissen,* and the Latin *video.* As applied to this oral tradition, Veda means "revealed wisdom," and the Vedic hymns are called *shruti,* or revealed truth. There are four divisions of Aryan Vedic literature:

The Rig Veda. Rig means "verse," and this Veda consists of verses praising the various deities of the Aryan pantheon. It contains 1028 hymns arranged into ten Mandalas, or cycles. The hymns are ascribed to *Rishis,* or seers, who received the revelations contained in them. This Veda is the foundation for the other three.

The Yajur Veda. This second Veda consists of a rearrangement of the hymns of the Rig Veda for use by priests in ordered worship. It also contains additional prose material, consisting of directions for detailed ritualistic services. It has survived in two forms, the White and the Black Yajur Vedas. The Black Yajur is older and contains much commentary; the later White Yajur is more systematic.

The Sama Veda. Basically the Rig Veda, rearranged with musical notations, for chanting, this has proved to be of but slight interest to the historian of religions.

The Atharva. The latest of the four Vedas (*arthavan,* "priest"), this departs from the Rig, has much prose rather than poetry, and consists mainly of spells and incantations. It is magical in purpose and reflects the popular religion of the late Vedic period.

THE VEDIC WORLD VIEW. The religious view found in these scriptures reflects the nature and ancestor worship found in most early cultures. Many of the deities addressed by the hymns of the Rig had their counterparts in Greek, Roman, and Persian religion. The world view is fairly simple, but some beginnings of metaphysical speculation appear.

The cosmos. Although the evidence is sparse, the world which the Aryan myths portray seems to have resembled the three-level universe found in the myths of Homer. The gods lived in the heavens, men on the earth below, and there was an underworld where the god of death and demons lived.

Deity. The forces of nature—of the sea, earth, and sky—are represented by a host of gods. Although polytheism prevails, certain gods are most prominent. Among the chief gods are Indra, both a war god and a weather god; Surya and Vishnu, both solar gods, Agni, god of fire, and Soma, god of the sacred soma juice, probably an intoxicating beverage made from a mountain plant. There was also a sky god, Varuna, perhaps akin to the Greek god Uranos.

In the later portions of the Rig Veda there is a strong tendency to combine the functions of the various gods into one supreme deity, but this is still incipient. There is no single creator god in Aryan religion: Dyaush Pitar, the Sky Father, is lord of gods, but several gods are addressed as creator, or Prajapati, "Lord of creatures."

Man. Man is a member of his tribe, born as nobleman, commoner, or slave, living as one who must be at peace with the forces of nature and fit into the life of his community. The main difference between the gods and man is that the gods are immortal, whereas men are claimed by death.

Man's plight. The forces which Vedic man faced and which threatened to overwhelm him were specific: disease, flood and famine, an early death, defeat in battle, and lack of success in the hunt. The causes of present disaster included the capricious actions of the gods, and failure to appease the ancestors (*pitris,* "forefathers") and gods with sacrifices, offerings, and prayers.

Salvation. To avoid disaster and to insure success, the Aryan sought help from the gods of nature and from his ancestors, offering them prayers and sacrifices of food and possessions; in time cultic practices were developed to make prayers and sacrifices more efficacious. This helps to account for the development of a priestly class (the *Brahmans*) whose duty it was to see that all necessary religious duties of the community were fulfilled. Some hymns, especially of the Atharva Veda, are pleas for help in attaining such goals as tribal prestige or success in love or gambling.

Conduct. There is no strong emphasis upon conduct, although right action is pleasing to the gods and therefore desirable. The concept of *rita,* that which is right or proper, may be defined as a cosmic order which applies both to men and to the gods. Varuna is addressed as a sky god who watches over the affairs of men and forgives ethical shortcomings. Essentially, however, ethical conduct in the Rig Veda is that which assures the peace and prosperity of the tribe and avoids the wrath of the gods.

Destiny. Aryan views about a possible life after death were not clearly developed, except for the idea of survival of part of the individual self after death. It was believed that the vital breath (*asu*) of the more important members of the society survived, but cremation of the gross physical body was practiced. Slaves and other property of a nobleman were burned with him, but his spirit survived in a paradise and lived with the gods, feeding on ambrosia.

VEDIC RELIGION'S SIGNIFICANCE. Reconstruction of the religion of the Vedic age is necessarily partial and inconclusive. From the standpoint of history, the Vedas present a religion at a simple level of evolution, with a polytheistic cult not unlike that of early Greece, China, or Mesopotamia. From the standpoint of Hinduism, however, the Vedas represent revealed wisdom; all later sacred writings are held to be in some way a commentary or more sophisticated expression of the truths already present in the Vedas.

CLASSICAL HINDUISM

RISE OF THE PRIESTLY CLASS. In early Vedic times, the tribal chief served also as religious leader, combining social, military, and spiritual leadership. As the cult became increasingly complex, those in charge became specialists, finally investing their own priestly traditions in a hereditary group known as *Brahmans.* Since it was believed that the prosperity and safety of the tribe depended upon the proper performance of an elaborate ritual, these Brahmans became more and more powerful, until they superseded the warrior chiefs (*Kshatriyas*) as the highest social class.

THE BRAHMANAS, OR PRIESTLY WRITINGS. The complex ritual, which developed in the late Vedic era far beyond the level reflected in the Sama, Atharva, and Yajur Vedas, has been preserved in a group of writings known as the *Brahmanas.* These scriptures, along with the four Vedas, are regarded as *shruti* (revealed truth); they consist of elaborate prose discussions of the meaning and application of the Vedas for sacrifice. Handbooks (*sutras*) which further systematized the Brahmanas were developed. A *sutra* (cf. "suture") strings material together in outline form for easy memorization.

THE FOUR CLASSES. By the middle of the first millennium B.C., four social classes, called *varnas* ("color"), were distinguished. A late Vedic hymn (Rig Veda X:90) tells how the four classes issued in turn from the head, arms, thighs and feet of the creator god, Brahma, at creation. They probably derived from social distinctions between the noble invading Aryans, the priestly functionaries of the tribes, and the commoners and conquered peoples. By this time, the priests had lifted themselves above the nobility.

The four classes are the *Brahman,* or priest; the *Kshatriya,* warrior or nobleman; the *Vaishya,* or commoner; the *Shudra,* or slave. The first three classes are called "twice-born," and the males are initiated into the religious traditions of *shruti* or Vedic truths (cf. Jewish bar mitzvah and Christian confirmation); they are invested with a sacred thread which is always worn to indicate this "second birth." But the Shudras are not allowed even to hear the sacred Vedas or to share in their message of salvation. (The Western word *caste* is of Portuguese origin [*casta,* "house" or "lineage"] and refers properly to the several thousand endogamous occupational groups which are loosely related to the four main classes.)

THE FOUR STAGES OF LIFE AND THE FOUR ENDS OF MAN. Just as society was ordered into four classes, the ideal Hindu youth was expected to develop through four stages (*ashramas*), and to have four proper goals. After investiture with the sacred thread a member of one of the twice-born classes was expected, in succession, to be a student; a householder with wife and children; a hermit meditating in the forest to seek enlightenment after renouncing, in later years, all family ties; a homeless wanderer (*sannyasin*), holy and freed from all earthly ties.

The permissible ends to one's striving were also four: to pursue *dharma* in order to achieve righteousness and virtue; *artha,* the practical end of material gain; *kama,* the goal of love, pleasure, and the aesthetic enjoyment of life; and finally, *moksha,* the goal of spiritual victory over life.

GROWTH OF SPECULATION AND MONISTIC THOUGHT. Along with the elaboration of ritual and sacrifice philosophical and mystical speculation arose. This sought salvation by the application of reason and intuition to the understanding of the Vedas. Although the Vedas continued to be the norm, their hidden and allegorical meanings were discussed and explored. The record of this approach to salvation is preserved in the Upanishads.

THE UPANISHADS. Although there is a large number of these writings the classical ones were produced between 800-300 B.C. The term *Upanishad* is given various meanings, usually being derived from the root *shad* ("to sit," cf. "sedentary") and the prepositions *upa* ("near") and *ni* ("down")—"to sit down beside." The term reflects the nature of these writings; they are essentially dialogues in which a teacher instructs a pupil. The principal Upanishads, for which the medieval scholars Shankara and Ramanuja wrote commentaries, number about a dozen. The Upanishads also are held to be revealed scripture; each is attached to one of the Vedas and also to a Brahmana commentary on a Veda.

The speculative thought of the Upanishads tends in the direction of a monistic world view in which all reality is derived from a single principle. As background for a description of this world view it is necessary to define several basic concepts. In Chapter Eight, the terms *samsara, karma,* and *nirvana* are explained. Other important terms follow.

Atman. This means "breath," as in "*atmos*phere," and also essential life, or soul. Each living being has an atman which is conceived to be a portion of a cosmic atman, the atman which is beyond (*para*) the world.

Paramatman. This cosmic spirit or breath is all that truly exists, all else being but a temporary manifestation of it. An individual's atman is temporarily separated from this world soul.

Brahman. This term, which originally meant a prayer addressed to a god, finally came to designate the ultimate god himself, the paramatman. Thus the neuter form of the word, brahman, or in combination, brahmanatman, refers to the cosmic spirit beyond this world of time and space. The term *brahma* is masculine, and therefore personal, and refers to the creator god, Brahma. A priest is a Brahman, often anglicized as Brahmin.

Maya. This is from *ma,* to measure; it refers to present space and time which are temporary, measured aspects of the infinite and eternal. This word came to mean the present world which is conditioned by space and time, and has but the illusion of permanence. Only the paramatman is unconditioned, being beyond maya, time, and space.

Punar-janman. Punar means "again," *janman* means "birth" (cf. "*gen*etics"). This is the doctrine of rebirth which holds that each individual has been *re*born into his present life from a round of previous existences.

Dharma. This is the law or duty which is binding upon a man according to his class, and depending upon his *jati,* "birth." It includes social and moral duty, and religious obligations. Since one's dharma determines one's whole life in society, it is regarded by some interpreters as the most important tenet of Hinduism.

Yoga. Akin to the English word "yoke," this means (1) to discipline or hold in check one's passions and physical nature, and (2) to yoke or link one's own atman with the paramatman, and thus cease to be reborn. The term *yoga* also came to be, like the word *dharma,* almost synonymous with religion. Thus the yoga that a Hindu follows is his path (*marga*) to salvation, just as his dharma is what he must do to fulfill his religious vocation.

THE WORLD VIEW OF THE UPANISHADS. With these key words before us, it now is possible to state the dominant world view of the Upanishads. It is based upon the assumption that all that truly exists is the brahmanatman, that this present world is maya, conditioned by time and space, and that the goal of religion is to free the atman of the individual from its cycle of rebirth.

The cosmos. The paramatman (world soul) alone explains all things. It is all that has ultimate existence; the world of time and space is maya, "measured out," for a brief time only. Ultimately all things come from, and return to, the paramatman, a reality beyond and above all human categories, but best likened to spirit or breath. Even though it is held to be without temporal qualities (*nirguna*), the most frequent descriptive phrase used for the paramatman is *sat chit ananda,* "being, intelligence, bliss."

Deity. The many gods of the Rig Veda are identified as but aspects of the paramatman. Thus Agni is the sun and Vayu is the wind; yet to one who knows, each is, in essence, the world soul. The world soul alone is eternal, yet is the cause of all maya things and exists unchanged forever.

Man. Man consists of an atman, reborn because of past karma into this maya world of time and space. He has a body and senses, but these are merely temporary maya aspects of his nature. His past karma determines into which of the four classes he will be reborn.

Man's plight. The Upanishads represent religion for the spiritual elite. It is assumed that most men will follow the traditional religion, being reborn again and again into maya existence. Some, however, restlessly seek that which is higher and for these few it is taught that man's present unhappiness and misery is caused by ignorance. It is ignorance to assume that this present world is of lasting value or meaning. The dialogues of the Upanishads seek to make possible a glimpse of the eternal in the midst of time, to teach the truth that, in contrast to maya existence, all that really matters is the paramatman. A man will be reborn continually until he recognizes this all-important truth. As for the mass of mankind, it will continue to pile up good and evil karma, and only here and there will an individual learn the true meaning of existence.

Salvation. This, as we have seen, has two levels. At the lower level, the average man follows his dharma or duty in accordance with his class. He is guided by the prescribed rituals and sacrifices to the gods and ancestors, and hopes to accumulate sufficient good karma to be reborn at a higher level in his next life. But the man of wisdom seeks to learn the one thing which, if properly grasped, would free his mind from ignorance and relieve his life from dependence upon good karma. This knowledge is found in the teaching, "Tat tvam asi." *Tat* means "that," *tvam* is the second person singular (thou), and *asi* is the corresponding form of the verb "to be." This phrase, "that thou art," teaches that the essential *you* actually is the real *that,* the paramatman. One's own atman *is* identical with the world soul. This knowledge enables one to cut through the ignorance which ascribes meaning and value to this world and makes possible an apprehension of the eternal in the midst of time and space.

Conduct. Two levels of teaching are also found for ethical living. The ordinary man will follow his dharma to insure good karma. This is motivated by desire to achieve a higher rebirth, and also by fear of a lower birth with accompanying misery. The informed man will also live a good life, but as one who has renounced ignorant and selfish attachment to maya existence. He will seek one thing, to know *tat tvam asi,* to know that his true nature is essentially one with the world soul. He will seek this knowledge by spiritual discipline, which eliminates all selfish actions, and by living a life which reflects his knowledge.

Destiny. The ultimate goal of the teaching of the Upanishads is first, to make possible the experience of *tat tvam asi,* in order to end the cycle of rebirths. This takes place when a man's individual atman loses its mistaken identity, its notion that it has a real existence in this world. True knowledge tears aside the veil of maya and the atman rejoins the paramatman, from which it became separated when it began its cycle of rebirths. Thus man's positive destiny is to achieve nirvana, to lose personal identity in the ocean of being.

The less fortunate, still ignorant or practicing evil karma, must be reborn into this world, or into a hell of punishment, or into a paradise of reward. But final cessation of rebirths comes only with true knowledge.

THE UPANISHADS' SIGNIFICANCE. This world view is the classical one of Hinduism. All later sects, heresies, and philosophies take their starting point from this position, either to build upon it or to disagree with it. Almost all Indian thought accepts rebirth due to past karma, and has as its goal the cessation of rebirth through prescribed action or special knowledge. Thus the famous Vedanta philosophy (Vedanta means "end or fulfilment of the Vedas") which in this century has won a wide hearing in the West, claims to teach the true interpretation of the wisdom of the Upanishads. On the other hand, the two heresies of the sixth century B.C., Jainism and Buddhism, although accepting Upanishadic teachings of karma and samsara, rejected other teachings, such as the reality of the paramatman and the notion that man possesses an atman which is a part of the paramatman.

Sectarian Hinduism

The development of the Upanishadic idea that knowledge is the way of escape from the cycle of rebirths led to the conclusion that there are two ways open to the seeker, but each way is restricted. This belief denies real hope to the mass of men, for the ancient way of Vedic sacrifice and priestly ritual had come under the control of the priestly class, the Brahmans. By 500 B.C., the belief was taking form that if one followed this "way of works" it was still necessary to be finally reborn as a Brahman in order to achieve nirvana at death. This meant that all non-Brahmans must endure at least one more rebirth before achieving nirvana.

The other way to nirvana, the way of knowledge of the Upanishads, also was limited, in this case, to those who had time for study and meditation; even then, salvation was experienced only by a select few, who perhaps had earned it because of merit from former lives.

But what of the great majority, especially those in the lower classes, who were doomed to the cycle of samsara, either because of low birth or because of the lack of opportunity for learning and meditation?

THE GREAT HERESIES; SECTARIANISM. The domination of religion by the Brahman class and its exclusive claims to religious superiority accounts, at least in part, for the rise of the twin heresies of Jainism and Buddhism.

The founders of these religions, Mahavira and Gautama, were both of the Kshatriya class, next below the Brahmans, and each of these reformers taught a way of release which was open, at least in theory, to everyone. But Jainism, because of its stress upon thoroughgoing asceticism, was restricted in practice to those few who were ready to renounce completely, not only the usual life of society, but almost all normal action. Buddhism, for its part, also made strict demands upon its followers, but with its teaching of a "middle way" between strict ascetisism and worldly indulgence, attracted a much wider following than did Jainism. Toward the end of the first millennium A.D., however, a combination of circumstances led to its virtual disappearance from India.

One of the contributing factors to the decline of Buddhism was the development of sectarian Hinduism and its cults of savior gods. Today, most Hindus follow one of the major savior cults, usually either that of Vishnu or Shiva. It is to a description of this popular Hinduism that we now turn.

SECTARIAN HINDUISM'S SCRIPTURES. The Vedas remain the basic revealed scripture of Hinduism, but there is a mass of traditions and writings which serve as guide to the faith and practice of the average Hindu. Whereas Vedic scriptures are designated *shruti,* or "revealed," these later writings are called *smriti,* or "remembered," and have the sort of relationship to the Vedas that the Jewish Talmud has to the Old Testament, or the writings of the Church Fathers to the Bible. Although most Hindus are illiterate, they usually are familiar with the oral form of these sacred traditions which serve as the basis for popular Hindu religion. The more important of them are:

The Laws of Manu. This collection of social and religious laws dates from about the time of Christ. The legendary author, Manu, was the first man, born of the god Brahma. These laws are in verse and describe in detail the rules for the "twice-born" or three upper classes. It is probable that the Code of Manu originated with a school of Brahmans known as the *Manavas.*

The Ramayana. "The story of Rama" is the older of the two main epic poems of India. A poem of 24,000 couplet verses, it is ascribed to the sage Valmiki, and in its present form comes from about the time of Christ. It tells how the god Vishnu manifested himself in the form of Rama, son of Dasaratha. In the story Rama is betrothed to Sita, who is abducted by the demon Ravana. The main part of the epic tells of the wanderings of the chief characters and of the help of the monkey-god, Hanuman, in the great battle to vanquish Ravana and free Sita. This epic is known all over South Asia, much as the Gospel stories are known throughout Christendom.

The Mahabharata. "The great Bharata" epic tells of early rivalries in the land of Bharat, i.e., India. In its present form it is a complex work. The main epic consisted of about 18,000 couplets, but additions of all kinds of legends, lore, and traditions have expanded it by some five times. It thus constitutes a prime source for knowledge of the popular religion of India. The main story concerns an ancient rivalry between two sets of cousins, the five Pandavas and the one hundred Kurus. The five Pandavas, of the house of Bharata, lose their kingdom to the Kurus by trickery, and the epic recounts their years in exile, their return to reclaim their kingdom, and the final, almost annihilating battle between the relatives. The battle is used as a framework for the famous *Bhagavad-Gita.*

The Bhagavad-Gita. "The song (gita) of the adorable one," sometimes called the "New Testament of Hinduism," is primarily a dialogue between the most famous fighter of the Bharata brothers, Arjuna, and his charioteer, Krishna, who reveals himself in the course of the poem to be none other than the god Vishnu, who has taken human form in order to reveal the way of salvation by *bhakti,* or devotion, to Krishna as Bhagavad, or Lord.

The Puranas. The term means "ancient tales." These contain stories about the gods Rama, Krishna, and others. They are favorites of Hindu villagers, being recounted by storytellers and teachers. These stories are basic sources for our knowledge of popular Hinduism; much of this material is regarded as erotic and even immoral by many non-Hindus. Two of the more important Puranas which have been translated into English are the *Vishnu Purana* and the *Bhagavata Purana.*

THE RISE OF PERSONAL GODS. As described earlier, the two classic ways of achieving nirvana, or release from rebirth, were restrictive rather than universal in scope. The way of Vedic ritual and sacrifice taught that only Brahmans were in their last birth; while the way of knowledge of the Upanishads was for the learned few. Thus a way of release open to all was needed. Another genuine need was for some outside help beyond man's own striving to gain nirvana. This double need was met by the way of salvation through devotion to a god, *bhakti-yoga.*

THE TRI-MURTI. "The three condensations," or manifestations of the paramatman, is a scholarly way of saying that, although the world soul itself cannot be truly known by those held in this maya existence, it creates, supports, and dissolves the universe by means of its three aspects, or *murtis.* These three are Brahma, the creator, Vishnu, the preserver, and Shiva, the destroyer. In these three modes, the unknowable paramatman is manifested so that man can call upon these personal forms of deity for help.

THE WORLD VIEW OF SECTARIAN HINDUISM. By building upon the earlier description of the classical world view of the Upanishads, we can now depict the way of salvation of popular Hinduism in our seven-point scheme.

The cosmos. The universe is vast, filled with innumerable worlds, heavens, and hells. The uncompromising monism of the Upanishads is modified by the teaching that there are tremendous cycles of creation and dissolution, each lasting some 4,320,000,000 years. To man, these are real and enduring cycles, but to the paramatman they are but momentary and meaningless episodes.

Deity. In practice, popular Hinduism is polytheistic; the hundreds of millions of villagers worship many local deities, fear numerous demons, and have neither a monistic nor monotheistic belief. The two gods,

Vishnu and Shiva, are very popular, and most temples and the major festivals stress the worship of one or both. The devotees of each god number in the scores of millions. (The third aspect of the Tri-murti, Brahma, is almost ignored in practice, perhaps because his role as creator involves the fact of rebirth rather than release.)

THE GOD VISHNU. Vishnu appears to have developed from a Vedic solar deity. The name is traced to the root *vish*, "to pervade." As preserver of creation, he manifests himself at necessary intervals by means of *avatars*, "descendings." The usual list of avatars gives ten, including one appearance as a giant turtle which lifted the earth above the primeval flood; another as Gautama the Buddha; but the two most important manifestations are as Rama and as Krishna, the heroes of the two great epics. Vishnu's wife is Lakshmi, or Shri, the goddess of fortune. His followers are estimated at about two hundred millions.

THE GOD SHIVA. Although the name *Shiva* ("auspicious") is not found in the Vedas and may be non-Aryan, this god appears to have the powers originally ascribed to the Vedic stormgod Rudra. Shiva has a twofold aspect. He represents male vigor, and is manifested through his sexual energy, *shakti*, expressed through his female consorts, Kali, Durga and others. He also is the patron saint of the ascetic and is represented as seated motionless, with matted hair, meditating, storing up untold energies. The worship of Shiva involves veneration of the symbols of the *lingam* and *yoni*, the male and female sex organs, and also fertility rites typical of an agricultural community.

Man. On the basis of past karma, man is reborn into a suitable class (Brahman, Kshatriya, Vaishya, or Shudra). Man has an atman, or *is* an atman, temporarily compounding a body out of three constituents, called *gunas* (threads). The three gunas represent the interacting of three qualities, *sattvas* (light, bright), *rajas* (inciting, passionate), and *tamas* (heavy, dark), to form the world and its inhabitants. Only the atman is eternal and unaffected by the cycle of rebirths.

Man's plight. Since Hinduism is a complex phenomenon, no simple statement on the cause and nature of man's plight is possible. Basically, it is linked with his rebirth into this world; no matter how successful and happy one is, he never can be completely so until he achieves release (*moksha*) from the cycle of rebirths. There are many corollaries to this basic conviction, however, and at different levels of society and in different religious traditions, grief and misery in this present life are ascribed to various causes. To many villagers, suffering occurs because the gods and demons have been offended or ignored. Again, there is the mythological tradition that the world is passing through a degenerate stage of history as the universe runs down toward its dissolution. The most important and constant theme in popular Hinduism, however, is that the root of man's misery lies in the failure to observe properly the dharma associated with one's birth and class. Since rebirth into a certain level of society is predetermined by karma, and must be accepted, any failure to follow rules of class, or in any way to flaunt them, is to court disaster, and indeed is the reason why famine, disease, and death stalk the land.

Salvation. Conversely, religious piety requires that class and its rules be followed and supported in every way to insure the highest happiness, prosperity, and long life, and the birth of many sons. One's dharma or law of life must be followed strictly. But at the same time, sectarian Hinduism offers several ways of salvation to man. In theory, there are three paths, called *margas,* which one can follow in the search for meaning and security in his present life and, if fortunate, to gain *moksha,* deliverance, at death. In practice, these often are mixed and followed concurrently, especially since the first is so basic to Hinduism that its practice is presupposed for most Hindus.

KARMA-MARGA, OR THE WAY OF WORKS. This is sometimes called *Brahmanism* because it advocates the following of the ancient Vedic rituals and priestly teachings. It also stresses following one's dharma. This path should guarantee happiness and prosperity in this world and the promise of a better rebirth.

JNANA-MARGA. The "way of knowledge" (cf. *gnosis,* "know") is, essentially, the way of life taught by the Upanishads, best known in the West as Vedanta. This way stresses knowledge of the transitoriness of this world and the identity of one's atman with the ground of being, the paramatman. This knowledge results in a life of peace and security in a world of confusion and change.

BHAKTI-MARGA. The way of devotion to a god, *bhakti* is from the root *bhaj,* which originally meant "to share," or give freely, and is the term for devotion to a god in the sense of complete trust and faith. The gods Vishnu and Shiva, and their avatars or female consorts are turned to with love, in the confidence that they will aid man in his present life. The classical expression of this religious devotion is the Bhagavad-Gita, wherein such doctrines as the following are to be found:

Krishna, the avatar of Vishnu, speaks to Arjuna—

> *"Whoever serve Me—as I show Myself—*
> *Constantly true, in full devotion fixed,*
> *These hold I very holy. But who serve—*
> *Worshipping Me, the One, the Invisible,*
> *The Unrevealed, Unnamed, Unthinkable,*
> *Uttermost, All-pervading, Highest, Sure—*
> *Who thus adore Me, mastering their sense,*
> *Of one set of mind to all, glad in all good,*
> *These blessed souls come unto me."* *

Here is something new compared to the old Vedic way of ritual, or the esoteric way of the Upanishads. By devotion to a god and trust in him, one can find hope, peace, meaning, help in this life, and for the life to come, the promise that one will abide in the god rather than be reborn.

Conduct. As has been indicated, one's dharma determines to a large measure one's right conduct in this world. The fear of social criticism for deviating from one's dharma is reinforced by the knowledge that one must avoid all evil karma or face rebirth at a lower level, or in a hell—or even be doomed to wander as a bodiless spirit through the meaningless corridors of the universe. In the way of devotion, *bhakti-marga,* however, one seeks to live a good life in order to please the deity. This makes it possible for a worshiper of Vishnu, for example, to accept his preordained lot, his low birth and menial vocation, and to fulfill his dharma, yet, by devotion to Vishnu, to transcend class and duty and find a higher meaning in his own life and conduct.

Destiny. Although the ultimate goal, in theory, would be to achieve nirvana, that is, the loss of the atman's individual identity by absorption back into the paramatman, most Hindu devotees desire *moksha,* or release, to be transported to the abode of Vishnu, or Shiva, and thus to

---

* *The Song Celestial,* translation of the Bhagavad-Gita by Edwin Arnold (London: 1885), chap. XII, lines 5-13.

share the god's divinity. As we have seen, one is reborn after death according to his accumulated karma, predicated both upon his previous class and upon faithfulness to his dharma. This rebirth might be at worst in a hell, or as a worm or other lowly or despised being. But it is ordained that in the end each atman will attain release from the cycle of death and rebirth.

PHILOSOPHICAL HINDUISM

Throughout history, most Hindus have been illiterate, learning the traditions of the epics, puranas, and other lore in oral form. But India also has produced some great thinkers, members of a literary tradition whose influence has spread far beyond her borders. Two outstanding medieval thinkers, who worked and wrote during the scholastic age of Europe, deserve mention.

SHANKARA (about 788-830 A.D.). Born in southeast India near Madras, Shankara opposed the waning Buddhism of his day and helped to revive Hindu theology. He founded schools and wrote extensively; his works include commentaries on the Upanishads and the Gita. He followed the Vedanta school and his system is known as *advaita* (undivided) monism. He taught *jnana-marga,* salvation by the path of knowledge. Although he accepted the idea of a creator god for the common man, he conceived of the ultimate deity as an impersonal entity without human or other qualities. His is the principal influence in current Indian philosophy.

RAMANUJA (about eleventh century A.D.). This theistic thinker stressed *bhakti-marga,* the path of devotion. Also from the Madras area, Ramanuja allegedly founded some seven hundred monastic centers and wrote commentaries on the Gita and other classics. In his qualified monism (nondualism), the Lord Vishnu is the source of all, but the individual self, when it achieves *moksha,* continues to have independent existence in Vishnu's care. Several important sects stem from Ramanuja. His position, that Vishnu has a personal concern for his created beings, has interesting parallels to the Christian doctrines of faith and grace.

THE SIX ORTHODOX SYSTEMS. Although many philosophical schools have existed over the centuries, by custom all are subsumed in the six main schools whose origins go back to pre-Buddhist times. They are called *Darsanas,* from a word meaning "seeing," which came to denote perceiving or teaching. They are orthodox in that, although they often do violence to the obvious and literal meaning of the Vedas, they accept their divine inspiration. They stress logical reasoning and cover every area of human thought. They are usually listed and studied in three pairs, each consisting of two schools, although this customary classification is mechanical and arbitrary. The three pairs are (1) Nyaya and Vaisesika, which actually stress analytical thinking, somewhat like modern logical positivism; (2) Sankhya and Yoga, which are dualistic in metaphysical presuppositions, assuming *purushas* (souls) and *prakriti* (matter) rather than the monism of the paramatman, and which undoubtedly influenced early Buddhism and Jainism; and (3) Purva Mimamsa and Uttara Mimamsa, or Vedanta, which deal respectively with man's dharma (duty) and with his ultimate nature.

Modern Developments in Hinduism

THE MUSLIM INFLUENCE. Although Muslim invaders conquered Sind, southwest of the Punjab, as early as 712 A.D., Islam did not become dominant in the Gangetic basin until the fourteenth century. The Quran's rigorous prohibition of idolatry led, over the centuries, to widespread destruction of Hindu temples and their glyptic art. Because of the Muslim destruction of temples, today it is only in southern India that ancient Hindu temples remain. One direct result of the spread of Islam was the rise of the Sikh movement, which is discussed in Chapter Twelve.

THE COMING OF THE BRITISH. In 1498, the Portuguese opened India to modern European trade and influences. But the most important European influence has been that of the British. In 1600, the East India Company was founded and rapidly expanded its influence over India, which had subsided into a group of feudal states with the waning of the Mogul empire (1526-1757). In 1757, Robert Clive won the battle of Plassey for the East India Company, and the British government took an increasing interest in India's political and economic affairs until the Sepoy Rebellion of 1857 led to that subcontinent's being declared a colony of England. Finally in 1947, three new countries arose as a result of the end to British rule: India, Pakistan, and Ceylon.

THE HINDU RENAISSANCE. European influences were revolutionary in India; they brought industrialization, Western science, education, and secularism. At the same time, Christian missionaries from Europe and the United States began an ambitious program to Christianize all India. Despite the existence of the Church of St. Thomas in south India, which claims to stem from apostolic times, and certainly is very ancient, Christianity actually had little influence until the nineteenth century, when it began to make significant advances in education and conversions.

These opportunities were welcomed by many Hindus. Ram Mohan Roy (1772-1833) led a reform movement to accept Western education and science and urged young Indians to attend Western universities. The Brahmo Samaj (Brahmo society) was organized to advance Westernization of Indian thought and education and to revitalize India's heritage. But others reacted negatively, and in 1875 the Arya Samaj was formed by Swami Dayanand Sarasvati (1824-83). This group stressed the revealed truth of the Vedas and called for a return to the ancient but purified Aryan way of life.

RAMAKRISHNA (1836-86). Born Gadadhar Chatterji, he founded a group teaching the unity of all religions; his disciple, Swami Vivekananda (1863-1902) visited America, where he lectured for about ten years, founded Ramakrishna missions, and spread Vedanta. In India, Vivekananda stressed social reform and the necessity to improve the economic and educational level of India, establishing schools, hospitals, and other institutions of mercy. In both India and America, the Ramakrishna movement has been heard sympathetically and has had influence out of all proportion to its relatively few adherents.

THE FUTURE OF HINDUISM. With India again fast becoming one of the great nations of the world, and with its population exceeding four hundred millions, its future is unpredictable. Caste restrictions have been outlawed by the central government; the actual results of such legislation, however, continue to be delayed by the slower pace of its acceptance in practice by Hindu society. With the rest of Asia, India is in the midst of revolutionary changes but with a rural population of over 80 per cent her ancient ways will change slowly. Hinduism continues to be the conservative and dominant influence in the life of her people.

Chapter Ten

JAINISM

The twin heresies, Jainism and Buddhism, arose during a period of great changes in India. The age was feudal; there was no real emperor, and the territorial limits of each feudal ruler were constantly changing. Two ways of salvation were dominant: the ancient Brahman way of karma-marga, based on the holy Vedas and the sacrificial cult; and the way of knowledge as found in the Upanishads. In addition, a new way, that of asceticism, had arisen, which required a severe disciplining of the physical body in order to acquire powers and achieve goals which others sought to attain through good works or meditation. It was believed that those adept at asceticism could see into the future, work miracles, visit heaven and have fellowship with the gods, and even experience the bliss of freedom from the limitations of time and space. Jainism is one of those schools of asceticism which has survived as a religion to modern times.

MAHAVIRA, THE FOUNDER OF JAINISM. The usual dates given for Mahavira are 599-27 B.C., although some date his birth in 540 B.C. His actual name was Vardhamana, but his followers use the title *Mahavira,* "the great man" or "hero," to designate him. Since the earliest written record of his life is dated about a thousand years after his death, and obviously is highly legendary in form, not much is known concerning him. In fact, his legendary career so closely resembles that of Gautama the Buddha that some scholars have claimed that they were one and the same, and it is apparent that the better-known story of the Buddha has influenced the tradition about Mahavira.

Cutting through legend, we learn that Mahavira was born in northeast India of the Kshatriya class, the son of a petty king. He married, and had one daughter. At the age of thirty, after the death of both parents, he renounced his family and inheritance, and for twelve years sought salvation. For the final thirteen months of his quest, he wandered completely naked, practicing the most austere asceticism. He finally experienced *moksha,* "release," the experience of blissful nonattachment to the world. Because of this, he is called *Jina* ("the conqueror"), and his followers are called *Jainas,* or *Jains.* He spent the last thirty years of his life teaching his doctrines and founding an order of monks, the *Sangha* ("congregation"). After his death, his followers continued to increase and, around the time of Christ, appear to have been an important group in India. Today they number about two million.

THE SCRIPTURES OF JAINISM. About one thousand years after Mahavira's death, in the sixth century A.D., a Jain council was held at the town of Vallabhi to collect the known oral and written traditions and to put them into canonical form. Although most of the earliest texts are lost, two main groups have been preserved; the Angas, or "limbs," and the Upangas, or "secondary limbs." Most are written in a late popular dialect of Sanskrit and contain sets of monastic rules, parables and stories, legends and myths. The more important have been translated into English. In addition to the canonical writings there exists a fairly large and important body of literature produced by the Jain community over the centuries.

THE WORLD VIEW OF MAHAVIRA. Although it is impossible not to read much later thought into the time and life of the founder of Jainism, the following emerges as the basic teaching of Mahavira. Jainism is labeled a Hindu heresy because it denies two of the basic orthodox beliefs of the age of the Upanishads: (a) the authority of the Vedas, and along with this the efficacy of the priestly sacrifices, and (b) the monistic teaching of the paramatman, and its corollary that man contains an atman which is part of the world soul. Instead, Mahavira taught a dualism akin to that of the Hindu Sankhya philosophy, the positing of two principles to account for the world and its inhabitants. At the same time, the Indian concepts of rebirth and karma were accepted, although the term *karma* was given a special meaning in Jainism.

The cosmos. Instead of the maya world of Hinduism, two eternal principles make up the universe. The first is called *jiva,* life or soul. There is an infinite number of jivas, each of equal and infinite worth. The other principle, *ajiva,* nonliving, constitutes the physical or material world. The universe might be imagined to consist of levels or layers of existence in each of which jivas dwell; at the lowest level life is evil and restricting; at a higher level is the world of animals and men; still higher, the world of gods or higher beings; and at the top, a state unconditioned by time and space in which free jivas live, all-knowing and blissful.

Deity. In the strict sense there is no deity in Jainism. What gods there are differ in no way from other jivas or living beings, except that they are temporarily living at the level of existence for gods. But each will be reborn at a higher or lower level until release from rebirth is achieved. And each god is a jiva who is responsible not only for his present, fairly fortunate state of existence, but also solely responsible for his ultimate achievement of moksha, or release. He can neither help others nor receive help in his cycle of rebirths. For this reason Jainism can be considered atheistic.

Man. Man is a jiva reborn into a real world of time and matter. He has a real body made up of different forms of ajiva, or matter. His rebirth and present level of life as a man are predetermined by karma, which has a special nature in Jainism. Karma, in this religion, consists of matter in a fine, atomic form which clings or sticks to a jiva soul; the more karma that clings, the heavier it becomes, and the lower one's rebirth; conversely, the being at a higher level of existence has less karmic weight to drag it down. Through all the series of rebirths which a jiva experiences, the jiva remains unchanged and unharmed by karma's clinging—just as a diamond is unchanged, whether it rests in filth, the stomach of a dog, or a platinum setting. Thus man's essential nature, his jiva, is in no way different from that of a jiva residing in rocks or roaches, stallions or gods. But each jiva has freedom to choose and learn how to change its present pitiable condition of existence, trapped in ajiva, time, and space.

Man's plight. Since in its free, untrammeled state a jiva is omniscient and blissful, man's plight is to have his true essence, his soul or jiva, trapped in existence and in the cycle of rebirths. In addition, any activity or thought causes karma to stick to one's soul, weighting it down. Although good karma does not cling too closely, it still enmeshes man in the world of time and matter, and all bad actions and thoughts add greatly to the burden of karma, causing him to sink deeper into the lower levels of life. Karma also increasingly clouds the initial brilliance and omniscience of the unburdened jiva, so that ignorannce also adds to man's present plight.

Salvation. Logically, if all thoughts and actions cause karma to stick to one's jiva, salvation could come only from ceasing to think or act. This seemingly absurd conclusion is actually followed: one is to do and think only what is absolutely necessary, and then only under the most carefully controlled conditions. Penance for wrong thoughts and acts, and the disentanglement of karma from one's jiva by strict asceticism, make it possible for a man to experience *kevala* (alone, solitary), glimpsing final release (moksha) while still attached to this world. He who thus sloughs off his burden of karma is called a *jina,* or conqueror.

Conduct. The ideal Jain way of life obviously is strict asceticism, in order both to avoid wrong thought and action in this life and to improve one's level of rebirth. Since the requirements are so strict, however, Jainism has two levels of adherents: the holy man (monk) and the layman. All Jains must take five vows: not to harm any living creature (*ahimsa*); to be absolutely truthful; not to steal; to be chaste in thought and deed; and to practice nonattachment to the world by the strict limitation of possessions. For the holy man, the last two require celibacy and poverty. Perhaps the main Jain contribution to Indian life is the teaching of ahimsa, a principle followed later by many Hindus, and made world-famous when advocated by Gandhi. Jains follow it to the extreme. Thus a monk will sweep a path, or a chair, with a soft brush before treading or sitting upon it to avoid harming even the tiniest insect; and hospitals for maimed and sick rats have been maintained. In addition to these five vows, the monk has thousands of detailed rules to follow, mostly extensions of the ideal behavior enjoined by the vows. The "three jewels" of right faith, right knowledge, and right conduct are stressed for all. The layman must avoid agriculture, since ploughing, for example, kills worms, hence most Jains engage in merchandising and banking.

Destiny. If one's jiva does not slough off all karma by the time of death, the remaining karma will cause a new linking of one's jiva with ajiva, and this will result in rebirth at a predetermined level. Since all bad thought and action cause karma to cling, suicide is forbidden, although one is allowed, under the most carefully prescribed conditions, to lie down out of doors and, by abstaining from food and drink, to allow death to come. For the Jina who dies freed from karma, the Jain nirvana, moksha (release) occurs. In this state, the jiva floats free of all attachments and enters the highest level of existence in which the jiva is blissful, all-knowing, and free from karma, never again to be reborn. Note that there is no union with a monistic principle as in Hinduism, but complete isolation of the jiva.

MAHAVIRA IN JAIN THOUGHT. Although Mahavira taught that man is his own best friend and neither needs nor can expect help from any divine being, he himself is held in high regard by his followers. The Jains refer to Mahavira as a finder of the way, a Tirthankara, and project this rule back into the dim recesses of time, positing a line of twenty-four such Tirthankaras, of whom the twenty-third was Parshva (about 750 B.C.), and the last was Mahavira. These "ford-finders" are revered by Jains and memorialized in temples and by giant statues, often naked, representing the saint as standing unmoving and uninfluenced by the world around him. Mahavira is revered as one of these saints, both as one who has shown the way and, to many Jains at least, as one whose influence can help one in the search for moksha.

JAIN SECTS. Although the history of Jainism is unclear, two main sects exist today which trace their origins back to about the beginning of the Christian era when, during a famine, a large group moved south from the Gangetic plain to Mysore. In the south, the strict practice of wearing no clothes, begun by Mahavira, was continued by the monks; but the group in the north began to wear clothes. The northern group is called the Svetambara (white-clad), the southern, Digambara (sky-clad). The latter do not admit women to their order.

JAINISM TODAY. The Jain community numbers about two million today, and owing to its tendency to stress merchandising and banking rather than agriculture, its members are, on the average, high in the economic scale. Education is emphasized and literacy is high; a strong tradition of Jain literature developed over the centuries. Today the Jains are treated by their Hindu neighbors much as another caste; they have both achieved influence and lived peacefully within the context of Hinduism.

Chapter Eleven

BUDDHISM

Buddhism is the oldest of the world's three missionary religions and has had much the same impact on Asia that Christianity has had on the West. Just as Christianity arose out of the matrix of Judaism, becoming a universal religion, while Judaism remained essentially identified with its own orthodox culture, so the message of Buddhism broke with those teachings of class and duty which have in large measure limited membership in Hinduism to those born into its community. All Asia has been influenced profoundly by Buddhist thought and practice. Buddhism is so widespread and has so many facets that it has been called a "family of religions" rather than a single religion. What follows is a simplified introduction to the more important aspects of Buddhist origins and the spread of its missionary work.

ORIGINS OF BUDDHISM

GAUTAMA, THE BUDDHA. The founder of Buddhism was born about 567 B.C., in the town of Kapilavastu in southern Nepal, about 100 miles north of Benares. His father was a petty ruler of the Kshatriya class. The Buddha-to-be was named Siddhartha, and since he was of the Gautama clan he often is called *Gautama*. The legends about his early life indicate that his followers believed he had renounced the greatest possible earthly security and splendor in order to discover the true way to salvation.

Gautama's traditional life-story tells how his father was informed by a seer at the birth of his son that Gautama was destined to become the greatest earthly ruler of history. If, however, he were to see four things —disease, old age, death, and a monk who had renounced the world— then the boy would abandon his earthly heritage to become the founder of a way of salvation for all the world. Gautama's father sought to keep his son from these experiences, so that he might pass on to him his kingdom. He built a great palace in the midst of a park and gave orders that neither the sick, the aged, a dead body, nor a monk should be allowed near the palace. The boy grew up shielded from the world and was married to a beautiful girl, Yasodhara, who bore him a son.

But the gods intervened and on successive days, as Gautama was being driven through his park, he saw first a man covered with loathsome sores and shaking with illness, then an ancient man tottering with age, a corpse being carried to its grave, and finally a mendicant monk in ochre robes whose appearance was peaceful and whose body was healthy. Gautama asked what each vision was, and when he was told, he began to meditate on the meaning of life and upon his new knowledge that each of us must grow old, may be wracked with sickness, and eventually must die. But the peaceful appearance of the monk helped him to make "the great resolve." It had already become common practice in India for a man to renounce his family and to seek salvation as a student and monk. We are told that one night there was a great feast with drunken revelry in Gautama's palace; finally, he alone was awake and sober. He surveyed the scene of debauchery and was revolted by its apparent meaninglessness. Then he decided to renounce forever his life of security, which also involved self-indulgence, pleasure, and material comfort.

He went to the door of his bedchamber, looked once upon his sleeping wife and son (called Rahula in the legend, meaning "bonds") and left the palace, never to return. Gautama shaved off his hair and put on the yellow robe of a mendicant, which was the same as the garb of the condemned prisoner who had forfeited all claims upon society.

The next part of the legend tells how he studied the Upanishads with the best teachers of the day, saw clearly beyond their message, and rejected it as unsatisfactory. He then tried the other way of salvation, asceticism, much like Jainism, for the stress was upon complete self-denial. He was so thorough in his practice that five monks began to follow him as their leader. Gautama became a living skeleton, but found that this way also did not suffice. The daughter of a herdsman came by and offered him a bowl of curds which Gautama ate. Because of this self-indulgence, his five followers forsook him as unworthy of their respect, but Gautama seated himself under a tree and vowed not to stir until he had achieved that for which he was seeking. For forty days and nights, during which Mara (death, or evil) sought to dissuade him from his quest, he meditated, and finally experienced the bliss of nirvana, of ultimate salvation. Whatever this experience was it is described as the act of becoming awake, *bodhi,* and at that moment Gautama became the Buddha, the one who had become fully awake, or enlightened. Buddhists believe that Gautama had lived many lives of strenuous striving to enable him, in his final rebirth, to achieve buddhahood.

After this tremendous experience, Gautama returned to the world and was met by the five monks who had vowed never to speak with him again. When they saw him approaching with a radiant appearance, all arose and paid him homage. He taught them the meaning of life and the way to salvation; then, he and they began to spread the message of the Buddha. An order of monks, the *Sangha,* was founded, and by the time of the Buddha's death, forty-five years later, the new religion had thousands of adherents.

THE SCRIPTURES OF BUDDHISM. Since Buddhism does not require orthodoxy in belief, there is no closed canon of scriptures. Accordingly, if all the Buddhist sacred writings were gathered together, they would fill hundreds of shelves. Nevertheless, there is an early body of scripture which is held as basic by most Buddhist sects, the scriptures of Theravadin or Hinayana Buddhism, known as the *Tipitaka,* or The Three Baskets. They are in the early Pali dialect of Sanskrit of northeast India. Tradition states that at the death of the Buddha, a council of five hundred elders was called to determine the accuracy of the teachings of the Buddha as preserved by the community. Probably there was no recording of oral traditions until about the first century B.C. The Tipitaka is therefore relatively late and may represent many centuries of composition and compilation.

THE TRIPITAKA. This name is the more common Sanskrit title of the Tipitaka, and refers to the form in which it appears as the basic scripture for the southern, or Theravadin, Buddhism of Ceylon, Burma, and south Asia. The three divisions are:

The Vinaya Pitaka is the basket or collection of discipline, consisting of the rules of the Order.

The Sutta Pitaka is the basket of discourses, of the dialogues between Buddha and his disciples on the teachings of the religion.

The Abhidhamma Pitaka is the collection of teachings on metaphysics.

The Tripitaka has been translated into English by the Pali Text Society of London; it consists, in Pali, of twenty-nine subdivisions within the three main divisions, and is almost ten thousand pages long. Although it began to take its present form only some four hundred years after the death of the Buddha, it is our primary source for his life and teachings.

THE TEACHINGS OF GAUTAMA BUDDHA. Like Mahavira, the founder of Jainism, Gautama was of the Kshatriya class and may have reacted against the Brahman teaching that only members of the highest Brahman class could hope to end the cycle of life without at least one more rebirth. In any event, the Buddha rejected the authority of the Vedas and Upanishads and denied the monistic doctrine of Hinduism that man has an atman which is of the same essence as the paramatman. He did accept the teachings of karma and of rebirth, but denied the position that this present world is maya (has no final reality). Instead it is probable that he taught that there is a plurality of souls or consciousnesses, called *purushas* (akin to the English, "persons"), as well as a real world into which purushas are reborn, there to live, suffer and die. His denial of the atman is called his "nonsoul" doctrine, but this appears to deny the monistic concept of the paramatman rather than to deny a self, or consciousness, which can transmigrate, or experience metempsychosis.

THE FOUR NOBLE TRUTHS. The knowledge which caused Gautama to become the Buddha, or the "enlightened one," is expressed in a sort of logical syllogism called the *Four Noble Truths.* They are presented here in terms of their meaning, rather than their scriptural context.

Suffering. This is the principle that the very fact and act of existing necessarily involves a person in suffering. "To live is to suffer" is an equation that teaches that birth, illness, decay, death, all are painful and full of suffering; to desire what we cannot obtain is suffering; to be separated from what we cherish is suffering. To lose an only child to whom one is attached is suffering; to desire fame and fortune and to fail to obtain it is suffering. This principle means that the cycle of rebirths itself partakes of the essence of suffering, since it means the continuation of existence.

The cause or origin of suffering. The cause of life, of rebirth, and of continued attachment to the world is *tanha,* or desire. It does not matter whether this is a craving for pleasure, security, or even for life itself, desire causes one to cling to the wheel of life, and this in turn causes rebirth; and, as has been said before, it is assumed that "to live is to suffer."

How to end suffering. Since to live is to suffer, and suffering is caused by desire, craving, then it follows logically that if craving were rooted out, suffering would be ended. So the third Noble Truth is that the Buddha has found a way out of the unending cycle of birth, growth, decay, death, and rebirth—by eliminating all desire, all craving, and thus bringing an end to the suffering which is existence.

The cessation of suffering. In order to eliminate *tanha* or desire one must follow the famous Noble Eightfold Path. The eight aspects of the path are difficult to render into an English which would fit the Buddhist context, but they are usually translated as (1) right views; (2) right aims or intent; (3) right speech; (4) right conduct or action; (5) right means of livelihood; (6) right effort; (7) right mindfulness; and (8) right meditation, or contemplation. This path leads to the cessation of craving and, finally, to nirvana, the cessation of rebirth.

THE MIDDLE WAY. If to live is to suffer, then the easiest way to cease to suffer would be to cease to exist, to commit suicide. For the Buddha, however, the very desire to cease to be was also a craving that had to be overcome. The Noble Eightfold Path was not to be that of complete self-denial, as was the way of the Jains. Instead, he taught a modified asceticism—the Middle Way—between self-indulgence, like that he had known as a prince, and the ascetic way of complete self-denial, which he had found to be useless.

THE WORLD VIEW OF BUDDHISM. When we turn to a description of Buddha's world view, we find him reluctant to discuss metaphysics. Like other religious leaders, such as Confucius, Socrates, and Jesus, Gautama stressed the need for man to understand his present lot rather than to speculate upon the origins and nature of the universe, or the nature of life after death. Any reconstruction of his metaphysics is actually a reading back into his thoughts of later points of view; there is therefore much disagreement on this matter among both Buddhist and Western scholars. At the same time, Gautama must have presented to his hearers a point of view with which they were familiar, just as Jesus, for instance, held a position close to that of certain Jews of his day. On this assumption, it would appear that Gautama rejected the monistic view of the world and man found in much of the thought of the Upanishads, but followed instead a dualistic position of the sort that later developed into the orthodox Hindu system known as *Samkhya.*

The cosmos. One possible interpretation of the Buddha's view of the cosmos, then, is that he taught a dualism of matter and spirit. Matter is called *prakriti,* a "making first," which constitutes the physical world. To prakriti is added a spiritual principle called *purusha* (person), and there is an infinite number of purushas. The world, therefore, is real, and a living being is a purusha fettered to existence in this real world.

Deity. Like Mahavira, the Buddha denied belief in any god who might influence man's life. But he undoubtedly believed in deities who lived in heavenly spheres; in fact in many of the stories of the Buddha's previous lives in the famous Jataka Tales, the Buddha appears in the form of a god. But no god is important to his scheme of salvation; no outside power can come to man's aid.

Man. Man is a spirit or purusha who has been reborn because of past karma into his present life. The prakriti (matter) which makes up his physical body is described in various ways. One refers to the various aspects of man's nature as *skandhas,* "aggregates," the constituent elements being *rupa,* bodily form, *vedana,* sensation, *samjna,* perception, *samskara,* "aggregate of formations," and *vijnana,* consciousness or thought-faculty. Another system of thought describes man's nature as composed of seventy-five *dharmas* or constituent elements. Both systems regard man as a phenomenon resulting from the causative factor of a karma-bearing purusha which acts as a sort of magnet to bring together real elements (skandhas or dharmas) to produce a temporary being. The original birth which began the wheel of life probably was caused by *avidya* (ignorance) and man is held to the cycle of rebirths, partly by ignorance, and partly by the *asavas* (fetters) of craving.

Man's plight. Man's very existence in a real world is his basic plight; this is caused, as we have seen, partly by past karma and ignorance, but is continued by *tanha,* craving. All desire and attachment to the world holds man in bondage to rebirth. His life is filled with fear, anxiety, hopelessness, and he is enslaved by the mistaken belief that he is an ego or true self as long as he is attached to this world in which to live is to suffer. The Four Noble Truths delineate the nature of man's plight for the Buddhist.

Salvation. The Fourth Noble Truth, the Noble Eightfold Path which follows the middle way between self-indulgence and extreme asceticism, is the Buddhist way to find meaning in a world characterized by suffering, and is the way to the cessation of craving and to passionless peace.

Conduct. Buddhist ethics rightly are admired for the total demand which they make upon the faithful. The Noble Eightfold Path stresses the necessity of right thought, speech, and action in every aspect of man's private and social life. This stress is made even more explicit in the five vows which are required of all who join the Sangha, the monastic order. These demand abstinence from killing, stealing, sexual immorality, lying, and the use of intoxicants and narcotics. The commentary on these vows makes clear that even the thought of hatred or lust is renounced. The Discipline of the Order contains many detailed rules and prohibitions to govern not only the practice, but also the most intimate thoughts of the monks.

The sanction and the motivation which prompt obedience to this high ethic is, of course, to be understood in connection with Buddhist teachings about the nature of man and his salvation. Although there is no god to obey, two compelling reasons support right conduct: the need to root out all self-centeredness or ego in one's life, and the desire to follow as closely as possible in the steps of the Buddha. Thus, we find that the teachings of the Buddha partake of the nature of the "divine" commands of some religions. In practice, if someone harms a Buddhist, and he answers violence with love, this represents, not primarily love for the other person, but rather the attempt to have no feeling of anger, resentment, or concern for self. For such attachments prove a person ignorant of the teachings of the Buddha or guilty of reluctance to follow in his path.

Destiny. When the Buddha was asked what happens after death to the monk who attains liberation, he answered that he had not attempted to answer this question. He had sought out and explained the causes of becoming—of birth, growth, decay, and death—and the way to put an end to this becoming. But what happens when one ceases to "become" he had not explained. The ultimate goal of the Buddhist is called nirvana, a term used earlier by the Hindus. For the Hindu, nirvana is a loss of individual identity by absorption of the atman into the paramatman from whence it came. The word "nirvana," as has been said, has two parts: the negative, *nir,* and *vana* from the root meaning "to blow." Thus one meaning of nirvana is "to blow out," and so to wane, to die away. Following the foregoing analysis of the nature of man's plight and his salvation, Buddhist nirvana can be understood as the waning of the tanha, the craving, desires, passions which serve to perpetuate the cycle of rebirth. Without the fires of craving, man's purusha would be liberated from all attachment to the world of prakriti. Two terms used to describe the experience of release while yet in this world are "to be cool" and "to be at peace."

Since the fate of the liberated after death was left open, Buddhists discuss a fourfold possibility or "tetralemma": after death the liberated being either exists or does not exist; if it exists, it is either conscious or unconscious. In the history of Buddhist thought, Buddhist philosophers have taken almost every conceivable position on that question.

THE THREE REFUGES. From earliest times, anyone who wanted to follow in the path of the Buddha to seek salvation and nirvana renounced the world and made his declaration of faith: "I go to the Buddha for refuge; I go to the Dhamma for refuge; I go to the Sangha for refuge." In this way, he declared his desire to become a follower of the Buddha, to seek to understand and follow the Four Noble Truths and the Noble Eightfold Path with its attendant dhamma (*dhamma* is the Pali form for Sanskrit dharma and in Buddhism means "religious law"), and to enter the fellowship of the Sangha and submit to its discipline. To this day, one who takes this step is striving to live as an *arhat* (*arhant*) or "worthy one." Those who feel that they are not ready, in this existence, to take the step of renunciation with its attendant vows of poverty and chastity may serve the arhants as lay members. Without the strong support of the lay community, the Sangha could not have survived; in fact such support was immediately forthcoming. Throughout Buddhist history, pious lay men and women of all economic levels have contributed generously, both to the Sangha and to mendicants, thereby gaining good karma which will aid them in their own spiritual pilgrimages through their cycles of lives.

THE DEVELOPMENT OF BUDDHISM

The great paradox of Buddhism is that a way of life that began with the teaching "to live is to suffer," and demands the rooting out of all desires and attachments to the world, should become a great missionary religion. The determination of Gautama, after his enlightenment, to return to the world and to preach his doctrine is, of course, regarded with gratitude by all Buddhists. The Buddha's compassion for the plight of all mankind, trapped in suffering and bound to the wheel of existence, proves how completely he transcended the level of ordinary beings. The religion which stems from his teaching has at least 150,000,000 active followers, and Buddhism directly influences the lives of most people in southern and eastern Asia. Although Buddhism actually can be described as a family of religions, it has two main divisions: the Hinayana and the Mahayana sects.

HINAYANA BUDDHISM. The earliest history of Buddhism is lost in the obscurity of legend. Tradition tells us that the first great council was held shortly after the Buddha's death to certify the accuracy of the doctrine and the rules of the Sangha. About one hundred years later, the Council of Vesali was held and by this time a number of sects had already developed and split over both doctrine and practice. The third council was held during the reign of the great Emperor Asoka (ruled about 269-32 B.C.) who supported Buddhism only after conquering much of the Indian subcontinent. By this time, the Theravada sect (school of the elders) was strong and developed the form of Buddhism which today is dominant in Ceylon, Burma, and Thailand. It claims to represent original Buddhism and stresses the way of the arhant, or holy man. Because of its emphasis upon nirvana as obtainable only by the few who follow strictly the way of the Buddha, it later came to be called *Hinayana,* the doctrine of the lesser way, or the lesser doctrine, meaning that only a few can pass to nirvana by this difficult way. This name was given it by its critics, but this sect prefers to be called Theravada Buddhism.

The Theravada movement reveres Gautama, the Buddha, not as a god but as one who has shown the way. It stresses the monastic life, and yet, paradoxically, from earliest times the monasteries have possessed great wealth and much land given by pious laymen, or by members taking the vow of poverty upon joining the order. In India, Buddhism proper died out by the time of the Muslim conquest of northern India (1200 A.D.). Many factors contributed to this disappearance of Buddhism in its original homeland, and one of them may well have been the concentration of men and wealth in monasteries where their vows of nonviolence made them an easy target for invading Muslims and other warlike groups.

Since our understanding of what the Buddha may have taught as his world view is based upon the Pali scriptures, we have described it earlier in this chapter. Today, Theravadin Buddhism is very active in southern Asia, has built beautiful temples and contributes to education in Burma and Thailand.

MAHAYANA BUDDHISM. The teachings of Theravadin Buddhism offer salvation and nirvana only to the arhant who has renounced this world. A man who marries and has a family and who seeks to earn a living as a regular member of society may become a lay follower of Buddhism, but he is excluded from those destined for nirvana. Because of this restriction, Buddhism lacked an essential ingredient of a missionary religion: the element of universality which offers hope to anyone, without restriction, who is seeking present salvation and final release. This element was supplied by Mahayana Buddhism which arose in northwestern India about the time of Christ.

Mahayana beginnings. By the time the "great vehicle" was well launched, its origins had already become obscured by legend. This school of thought claims that the Buddha taught an inner circle of his followers a higher tradition, not recorded in books but offering hope to all. In fact, however, this school seems to show the influence of ideas from the West, especially from Zoroastrianism and from Greek thought, and in its development of savior gods and concepts of heaven and hell to reflect aspects of Hindu polytheism and cosmology.

The Bodhisattva. Although the Buddha himself seems to have taught that there are no gods who can help man in his search for release, one of the distinctive characteristics of Mahayana is the Bodhisattva, a being whose "essence is enlightenment." Gautama probably believed that he himself had struggled for many millenniums, through many births, before he finally achieved the victory of buddhahood. After his enlightenment, he did not immediately enter nirvana but instead returned to society and, for forty-five years, taught his doctrine. Perhaps it was only logical that his later followers should teach that even after his death he had not completely deserted mankind. In any case, the doctrine of Bodhisattvas allows for many such beings as Gautama, the Buddha, who have been victorious and achieved buddhahood, but who still are available, as helpers, to those who call upon them in faith. These beings have taken a vow that they will not enter nirvana until the last sentient being has attained it. Thus, by incorporating into its scheme the local gods of the different areas of Asia, Mahayana Buddhism has become a religion of savior gods. Because saving help is thus available, the devotee can remain in the usual way of life while continuing on the path to nirvana; he need not depend upon his own efforts to obtain release.

Changing concepts of nirvana. The other important development which made Mahayana appealing to masses of followers, instead of just the few monks, was its idea of life after death. Instead of the agnostic position which Gautama took, many Mahayana sects introduced a whole panoply of heavens and hells. The difficult concept of extinction at death, or at least the blank wall of agnosticism, has never been popular with large numbers of people. Hinduism and even primitive teachings such as the Bøn religion of Tibet, had ready-made, for Buddhist adaptation, heavens and paradises for the faithful. Once again, a universal position was taken by the Mahayana, as opposed to the more limited position of the Theravada.

BUDDHISM AS A MISSIONARY RELIGION

Gautama himself appears not to have foreseen that his teachings would become the source of a full-scale missionary religion with savior gods, saints, and elaborate temples. But today Buddhism is a vital force, not only in Asia, but also in Europe and North and South America, especially in urban centers. Following the pattern for missionary religions outlined in Chapter Six, the three basic elements of the missionary dynamics of Buddhism are analyzed here.

BUDDHIST UNIVERSALISM. Buddhism, like Christianity, broke with its mother religion, Hinduism, basically over the question "Who can be saved?" Hinduism taught rebirth, based on past karma, into a fore-ordained class and only those reborn into the highest, the Brahman class, were believed to be able to achieve nirvana. The Buddha taught that anyone who accepted the Four Noble Truths and followed the Noble Eightfold Path could hope to achieve buddhahood and nirvana. His radical definition of the human situation—to live is to suffer—is true of all in this world, and if the Buddha's presuppositions about karma and rebirth are accepted they are equally universal. Neither birth, color of skin, nor any other human consideration or barrier prevents men from following the path of the Buddha. Its racial tolerance is of increasing importance for the future of Buddhism at the present time.

The claim that Buddhism is universal must be qualified, for it is tacitly assumed in both Theravadin and Mahayana teachings, that one who achieves arhantship or bodhisattva qualities in this life has earned this position through many previous good lives. A spiritual aristocracy, therefore, is assumed. The position of women, too, qualifies the universality of Buddhist teaching for it is implied that men are superior and that women are further from buddhahood. This attitude probably reflects, first of all, Indian and Chinese cultural assumptions and also is a corollary to the notion that previous lives are rewarded by rebirth at higher levels. In a culture where men are assumed to be superior to women, their spiritual superiority is implicit. In practice, however, Buddhism has always accepted women in the Sangha, and the early *Psalms of the Sisters* contains ample testimony of feminine experiences of nirvana.

THE CONTINUITY OF BUDDHISM. Any religion which spreads over large areas and beyond its country of origin must have strong elements of continuity, binding it together and preventing it from becoming dissipated and from being absorbed into other cultures. At least four such aspects of Buddhism are noteworthy.

Buddhism's continuity with Hinduism. As noted earlier in our discussion of the career of Gautama, the founder of Buddhism accepted many elements of Hinduism, even though he rejected the authority of the Vedas and the doctrine of a world soul. He accepted rebirth as determined by past karma, and his message was addressed to Hindus. Thus, Gautama could base his teachings upon certain aspects of Hinduism and his early followers could understand his message in the context of their pre-Buddhist faith.

The Buddha. From the beginning of their religion, all Buddhists have repeated, as the first of three declarations of faith: "I go to the Buddha for refuge." Time and space are thus transcended for all Buddhists. Whether one considers third century B.C. India, second century A.D. Ceylon, seventh century A.D. China and Tibet, tenth century A.D. Japan and Korea, or twentieth century Hawaii, London, or Paris, all Buddhists have in common their loyalty to the person of the Buddha. Even though each believer may have his own interpretation of the Buddha's nature, the Buddha's person provides a solid basis for continuity.

The Dhamma. All Buddhists also affirm "I go to the Dhamma for refuge." For the Theravada Buddhist, this phrase, of course, means specifically the rules of the Sangha. But the law also represents the common adherence of all Buddhists to the teachings of the Four Noble Truths and their acceptance of at least the minimum of Buddhist ethics and doctrine. For most Buddhists, this Dhamma is found in the Tripitaka, the basic scriptures of Buddhism.

The Sangha. The third affirmation of the Theravada Buddhist is

"I go to the Sangha for refuge." The Sangha, or order of monks (there also is one for nuns), which was begun during Gautama's lifetime, has had a varied history. In the Theravada countries, the history of the order has been fairly peaceful, whereas in China, Buddhist monks often have been the victims of greedy rulers or of persecution by Taoist and other Chinese cults. In contemporary Tibet, a large percentage of the male population belongs to monastic orders; these are an easy target for Communist domination.

Although in Mahayana countries, it is not necessary to enter an order to attain release, even in these countries the Sangha does represent a genuine element of continuity, both historically and geographically.

BUDDHISM'S ADAPTABILITY. As well as the elements of universality and continuity, a missionary religion must possess a certain degree of flexibility. Hinduism and Judaism today represent the rigidity of religions which, over the centuries, have more and more tended to identify with a culture, and have stressed parentage as the way of entering the religious community. As a missionary religion moves into new countries and faces new cultures and situations, its message of universalism must be tempered by the ability to adapt to new situations.

Buddhism has not only been adaptable to new situations, but probably has been too much so. The Bodhisattva has been interpreted so broadly that the pre-Buddhist gods and goddesses of a country are often identified with past incarnate Buddhas. In China, for example, the goddess of mercy, Kwan Yin, became an important Bodhisattva. In Tibet and neighboring areas, the temporal ruler has been hailed as the incarnation of a past Buddha and revered as a living god.

The Buddhist teaching, "to live is to suffer" has also tended to result in a lack of concern for improving social and economic conditions. Education, hospitals, better treatment of slaves or laborers are all of little value in a world from which one seeks escape. There also is a lack of concern for orthodoxy that often is interpreted to the West as tolerance. There is a Buddhist dogma that eventually every sentient being will achieve release from the round of rebirth. Since this is so, it is only a matter of time before any particular being achieves buddhahood. It does not matter what anyone believes; it matters only that he strive to do his present best. If one chooses to take seriously the Buddha's teachings in this life, well and good. But if not, there are many more millenniums and many more lives during which one can learn and follow the truth.

Buddhism has none of the urgency of decision and commitment which is characteristic of the other two missionary religions, Christianity and Islam.

THE WORLD VIEW OF MAHAYANA BUDDHISM. In practice, this easy adaptability of Buddhism makes it somewhat amorphous: it lacks any monolithic structure with clear-cut membership requirements or dogmatic tests for membership. Today there are no real membership figures for Buddhism nor any concern that records be made of numerical strength. It is also true that a Buddhist can mix, or practice side by side, one or more religious commitments or philosophies. Thus in China, one might follow certain Taoist practices as a farmer, obey Confucian teachings in his social life, and at the same time consider himself a Buddhist in such matters as funeral services or prayers for help in time of sorrow. Hence, it is difficult to characterize Buddhism sharply in terms of either historical development or geographical spread. At the same time, certain beliefs or teachings appear to be basic to Mahayana Buddhism; again, therefore, we present our seven categories of religious ideas (much of it already stated, but repeated here in order to fill out our scheme) and then comment briefly on Buddhism in Tibet, China, and Japan.

The cosmos. Although Gautama refused to discuss metaphysical questions, his followers through the centuries have produced thousands of documents on the nature of the physical world and the world of the spirit. The greatest single change from the realism and dualism of Gautama is the notion of escape from the confines of time and space. This frequently involves a kind of monism, or idealism, in which the concept of nirvana becomes not extinction, but "the void," emptiness, the unconditioned. Thus alongside the popular cosmologies of the peoples of Asian countries, Mahayana presents, in various forms, a monistic concept not far removed from Hindu Vedanta. All that is truly important is declared to be timeless, and, except under rare circumstances, ultimately unknowable whereas the world is held to be transient and perishing.

Deity. Gautama denied that there are any gods who can help man, but the Mahayana doctrine furnishes a whole pantheon of savior gods. Again, it probably is from Hinduism that this basic pattern is derived. Later Hinduism teaches three levels of divine beings. The highest is the paramatman, or world soul; next is the level of the Tri-murti, or secondary manifestations of the ultimate; and finally the incarnate sav-

ior gods, or avatars, who live among men for their salvation. We find
in Mahayana thought a close parallel to this scheme in the three levels
and three bodies of the Buddhas:

THE DHYANI BUDDHAS. These possess a *dharma-kaya,* or absolute
body. They are "Buddhas of meditation" and have entered nirvana forever, never again to have contact with the world of space and time. This
corresponds to the paramatman of Hinduism.

The bodhisattvas possess a SAMBHOGA-KAYA, body of bliss. This corresponds to the level of the Hindu god, Vishnu, for though they reside in
paradise they have power to come to the aid of men.

THE MANUSHI BUDDHAS, or human Buddhas, possess a *nirmana-kaya,*
or body of transformation. These Buddhas have lived among men, as did
Gautama, and are comparable to Krishna as the avatar of Vishnu. Once
a manushi Buddha has performed his allotted task he enters nirvana and
is beyond the prayers of men.

Although this view of deity is somewhat scholastic and would be as
difficult for the average Buddhist to comprehend as the Christian doctrine of the Trinity is to the average Christian, it is basic to much of
Mahayana theology.

Man. The Four Noble Truths teach that to live is to suffer. Man is
a sentient being, of a high level, who is reborn because of past karma.
He is trapped in time and space, and his true purpose is to escape
this cycle of rebirth. In practice, the Buddhist doctrine of man would
also reflect and incorporate aspects of the views of man held by the society in which the religion is practiced, whether Chinese, Japanese, or
Burmese.

Man's plight. Since man is caught in the round of samsara, the greatest single cause of his present sorrow is ignorance—ignorance of the
causes of his rebirth and also of the nature of that ultimate truth which
transcends time and space. Any clinging to life, any attachment to the
world which attributes importance to transient things, causes misery and
prolongs existence.

Salvation. This has at least two levels. The lower level offers man
help if he turns to Bodhisattvas, beings who have achieved buddhahood
but have refused to enter nirvana until all sentient beings precede them.
The second level parallels that of the way of knowledge in Hinduism.
Its meaning is expressed in the famous chant, "Om mane padme om."
Literally this means "Om, the jewel is in the lotus, om." The syllable

om (Sanskrit, *aum*) has a symbolic meaning. The jewel represents the hard, clear diamond of eternity, of timelessness. The lotus represents the beautiful flower which suddenly blossoms on a pond and as soon fades and decays. This is time, samsara, attachment to the transient beauty of the world. But in the midst of time and space, eternity is to be found by those who follow the path of knowledge and learn the true meaning of existence. They can experience the peace of nirvana in the midst of time. "Om mane padme om."

Conduct. Mahayana Buddhism stresses a high order of ethical living. Although this sect does not require that one completely renounce the world, it does stress nonattachment and selflessness. The Dhamma-pada, a scripture summarizing the path of the law, is widely taught. Faith in a Bodhisattva also carries the notion that one should do good, not only to acquire good karma, but also to be pleasing to the savior god.

Destiny. At the higher levels of Buddhist thought, the agnosticism of Gautama concerning the state after death is replaced by a view of nirvana which avoids the obvious limitations inherent in a completely negative description of the arhant's destiny. Although nirvana is still defined as a waning away of the self, and is sometimes referred to as a *void,* this void has certain desirable qualities ascribed to it. Thus, nirvana is an existence, but it is not bound by time or space and does partake of bliss and omniscience. Cessation of samsara, complete severing of attachments, loss of selfhood, the ending of processes of becoming, are all accompanied by the promise of eternal bliss.

Buddhism inherited from Hinduism the doctrine that rebirth, and possible intervening existence in hells or temporary heavens, is the fate in store for those who do not, in this existence, achieve nirvana. In each area into which Buddhism has moved, the content of such hells and heavens was supplied from the earlier, pre-Buddhist beliefs of the people. Since even "eternity" is probably a relative term to the unsophisticated mind, the promise of a heaven of bliss, where one can be with Bodhisattvas, far removed from the terrors of both life and death, is easily accepted by many as the ultimate destiny. Thus in China the Ch'ing T'u, or "pure land" sect teaches that, if one has faith in the Bodhisattva Amitabha ("unmeasured light"), and repeats in faith his name, at death, Amitabha will take the faithful to the pure land of bliss to remain there with him forever. In Japan, the name was transformed to "Omitofu" and the sect called *Jodo.*

BUDDHISM TODAY

The history of the Sangha and of Buddhist thought for the past 2,500 years must be read elsewhere, but a tribute to the contribution of Buddhism is in order here. This missionary religion has not only raised the spiritual level of barbaric countries throughout South, Southeast, and East Asia but has also been a primary influence in Asian art, literature, and education.

Our century has seen a genuine resurgence of Buddhism throughout the world. In 1907, the London Buddhist Society was founded, and the translation and publishing of Buddhist texts which it has sponsored have helped to make the entire West aware of the riches of Buddhist thought and religion. In southern Asia, this renaissance has been represented by the 1954 Buddhists' World Council, attended primarily by those of the Theravada following. In East Asia, Japan is presently the center of Mahayana, in spite of attempts during the past hundred years to replace Buddhism with Shinto. Since the granting of statehood to Hawaii has added tens of thousands of Buddhists to the number of voting citizens, Americans are becoming increasingly aware of the message of Buddhism.

Chapter Twelve

SIKHISM

Northwest India was invaded by Muslims for the first time in 712 A.D. For the next thousand years, Islam menaced Hindu rule. Although it dominated political affairs, especially in North India, until the British occupation, Islam never completely supplanted Hinduism nor did it completely destroy the culture of India. In the fifteenth century, Hindu reaction and resentment began to gain strength and direction, and several significant reform movements arose. The reforms, although reflecting much of Muslim criticism of Hinduism, opposition to idolatry and polytheism, and condemnation of caste, infanticide, and suttee, were basically Hindu in spirit and direction.

One reformer was a Muslim rug weaver of Banaras named Kabir (c. 1488-1512) who deplored the strife between the two religions and taught that Muslim and Hindu alike were brothers under the fatherhood of God. Much of his teaching has been preserved, and he would appear to be typical of a number of leaders of the period. One of his followers was Nanak, the founder of the religion of the Sikhs.

LIFE AND TEACHINGS OF NANAK

Nanak (1469-1538 or 1539) was a Hindu born into the Kshatriya class, in the Punjab village of Talwandi, near Lahore. He is reported to have been a quiet, sickly boy with little desire to engage in trade or to follow the usual pattern of life. He married and had two sons, but soon left home, renouncing his family. According to legend, at about the age of thirty-six he had a mystical experience, visiting heaven, where he was addressed by a divine being and offered a drink of nectar. He was told that the god who addressed him was Brahma, the primal being, and that Nanak was to repeat Brahma's name and teach others to do the same.

Nanak began to teach a new doctrine, proclaiming his god and saying that "there is no Hindu and no Muslim." He traveled widely with a

Muslim musician, Mardana, making at least two important missionary journeys. He attracted followers throughout the Punjab and also in such places as Bengal and Ceylon; legend tells of a visit to Mecca and the Ka'ba, where he made a dramatic impression upon Muslims. At the time of his death in 1538 his following was strong, and since he felt that his two sons were unworthy to succeed him, he appointed a disciple, Angad, to become the second human Guru, or teacher.

THE WORLD VIEW OF SIKHISM. Nanak sought to achieve harmony between Hindus and Muslims by teaching a religion of reform which would be true for all men. It is called the religion of the Sikhs, the "disciples" or followers of the Guru. Nanak opposed the religious authority of the Vedas, and probably also that of the Quran. From Islam, he adopted the teaching of one true god for all people, without regard for social or economic class. He opposed Hindu teachings of class and caste, but accepted its teachings of karma and rebirth, of maya, and of a pantheistic or monistic deity. Under our seven-point scheme his teachings can be analyzed as follows.

The cosmos. This basically is in the context of Hindu presuppositions. There is a monistic principle underlying all existence, though it is described in personal terms. The present world of time and space is transitory and any serious attachment to its values is vain. In this monistic context, the world of time and space was created by the deity for his own purposes.

Deity. The god proclaimed by Nanak, though the sole cause and principle of existence, is conceived in personal terms. He is called *Hari* (a designation for Vishnu in Hinduism, just as Kabir called his god Vasudeva, another Vishnu bhakti epithet); he is called Guru, or the true teacher; he also is designated by the term *Sat Nam,* or True Name. He is, for all men without distinction, the one true god. Here the emphasis is not upon class or caste but upon the equality of rich and poor under Sat Nam, who is creator of this present world and the source and goal of all life. In harmony with Muslim teachings, Nanak's god has no incarnations and cannot be represented by idols.

Man. The syncretism of Hinduism and Islam continues in Nanak's doctrine of man. Following Hindu thought, man is reborn because of the influence of past karma, but his essential nature contains a part of god. Yet, following Muslim thought, man is god's creation whose duty it is to please his creator, and there is no distinction of birth or class to be made between men. Though man is called upon to serve Sat Nam, we find also the Muslim teaching of Kismet, that is, that man's fate is completely in the hands of the deity.

Man's plight. Like Hinduism, Nanak taught that man's plight involves rebirth into this world and separation from god by evil thoughts and deeds. Unlike Hinduism, he ascribed man's present troubles, first of all, to disobedience to the demands of his god or to ignorance of his demands. Though man is expected to obey his creator, Nanak's emphasis is upon sins of sensuality rather than upon willfulness as the source of alienation.

Salvation. Nanak taught that present salvation is to be sought in submission to the will and purpose of god. But this requirement, which reflects Mohammed's concern, is buttressed with a clear doctrine of grace. This is in the context of Hindu bhakti, of devotion to a personal god. This acceptance of god's grace involves some activity on the part of the devotee. One must follow the current Guru, or spiritual teacher, to learn the truth about god, and also constantly to repeat one of the divine names, Hari, or Sat Nam. To do so will keep one's thoughts and actions close to god.

Conduct. The Sikhs are meat eaters in the midst of vegetarian Hinduism, for Nanak opposed asceticism and world denial. So they became a sturdy people and their strength stood them in good stead when persecution became severe in the seventeenth century. Prohibitions against tobacco and intoxicants, and an emphasis upon a natural married life, reflect Islamic teachings and have also contributed to the vigor of the Sikhs. Desire to please Hari and to live with all men as brothers gave a strong pacifist coloring to early Sikhism, but this was modified, and in later years, the Sikhs even became strongly militaristic.

Destiny. Rebirth is fated for those who do not believe or who are not saved by Hari's grace. Reunion with god is the true fulfillment of life and the desired destiny. There is no belief in the Last Day—the eschatology—of Islam. Instead, the Hindu concept of nirvana is reflected in the teaching that the soul of the redeemed will merge with god.

The foregoing analysis partially demonstrates the merits of the contention that Nanak's doctrine is more a reform of Hinduism than a true syncretism of Hinduism and Islam. It is indeed a reaction against

Islam, utilizing such positive aspects of Islam as opposition to idols and caste, but seeking to recover and stress the best in Hinduism as Nanak knew it, especially the bhakti emphasis upon a personal god of grace.

THE RELIGION OF THE SIKHS

THE SCRIPTURES OF THE SIKHS. The Sikh term for their scriptures is *Granth.* In early Sanskrit this term means "knot," and refers to the knot in the thong which held together a palm-leaf manuscript to form a crude book. Later it came to mean "book." The *Granth* sometimes is called the *Adi Granth* ("First Book") and also the *Sahib Granth,* or Lordly Book. This scripture was compiled by the fifth Guru, Arjun, who was the fourth in succession to Nanak. From 1581-1606, he headed the reform movement. Arjun brought together the teachings of Nanak and of the Gurus immediately succeeding him, including their hymns and prayers. He also included in the Adi Granth traditional materials from early bhakti teachers before the time of Nanak, as well as stories and legends of many Sikh teachers which had become part of the oral tradition of the movement. This book, the Adi Granth, was compiled for the benefit of the believers, to furnish them with scriptures to compete with the Quran and to strengthen their faith. Later, the Granth took the place of the succession of Gurus and is today regarded as the earthly Guru, guiding the followers of Hari.

The tenth and last Guru in the tradition also compiled a lesser scripture known as the *Dasam Granth,* or Granth of the Tenth (Guru). It contains a militaristic emphasis, added to strengthen the religion in its fight for survival.

Arjun, the Fifth Guru, employed a special script, which had been developed by the second Guru, for the composition of the Adi Granth. This alphabet is called *Gurumukhi,* or "mouth of the Guru." The main language of the Granth is Hindi, but it contains half a dozen languages, and even more dialects. It is therefore not comprehensible to most Sikhs; despite that fact, they hold it sacred.

THE GURUS. There were nine Gurus in succession after Nanak, making ten in all. There is not room to list them all, but several deserve attention, especially the last, since he changed the whole direction of the religion. The second Guru was Angad whom Nanak appointed to suc-

ceed him. Angad's most important achievement was the development of
the Gurumukhi alphabet.

We have already mentioned the fifth Guru, Arjun (1581-1606), who
compiled the Adi Granth. Arjun supported a rebellion against the Muslim ruler, Jahangir and, when the revolt failed, was tortured to death.
He was the first martyr in Sikh tradition, but soon there were many
more. The Indian nationalistic fervor of the Sikhs caused them, again and
again, to take the side of those fighting the Muslim Mogul oppressors,
and usually they were defeated. This continued conflict, however, served
to weld the Sikhs more closely together and to develop a militaristic tradition.

The tenth Guru was Gobind Rai, 1675-1708. His father, Guru Teg
Bahadur, was executed by a Muslim ruler, and Gobind Rai soon organized the Sikhs into a definite military order, both for self-protection and
to spread the faith. He took the name Singh, meaning "lion," and con-
ferred this title upon his followers. He organized his followers into the
Khalsa, or brotherhood of the pure, and instituted a rite of baptism with
a sword and nectar (sweet water). Each member of this military order
of the Khalsa was ordered to wear the five K's: the *Kesh* (hair, which
is never cut), *Kach* (trousers), *Kirpan* (dagger), *Kartha* (iron brace-
let), and *Kanga* (comb). He welded his followers into a powerful fighting force, but it was many years before the Sikhs achieved a measure of
peace with their Muslim rivals. Since his own sons were killed in battle,
Gobind Singh decreed at his death that henceforth the Granth would
take the place of human Gurus.

Although Gobind Singh's dramatic measures did help the movement
to survive, the spiritual level of the community appears not to have fared
so well. Today, some measure of idolatry is reported among the Sikhs.
In addition, reverence for the Granth, a copy of which is revered in the
Golden Temple at Amritsar, has replaced the vital tradition of the
teachers, and Hinduism continually nibbles at the fringes of the movement.

Sikhism Today

The fourth Guru, Ram Das (died 1581) established a temple at a
pool called Amritsar (immortality). Today, the city of Amritsar in the

central Punjab is the political and religious capital of Sikhism. In the partition of India in 1947, the line between Pakistan and Hindustan was drawn practically through Amritsar, and it became the center of bloody riots and slaughter. The Sikhs were caught in the middle of this holocaust and contributed their share to the resulting chaos. Today there is an uneasy peace in the area; the Sikhs are seeking to find their place in the new order which is still arising out of the agony of the division of India. Their tendency has been to side with the Hindus rather than with the Muslims and the country of Pakistan. There are about six million members of the Sikh community, and like other religious or language groups in India, they desire the creation of a separate state, Sikhistan; thus they hope to establish a political basis for religious tolerance and brotherhood.

Part Four

THE RELIGIONS OF
CHINA AND JAPAN

Chapter Thirteen

ORIGINS OF CHINESE RELIGION

China boasts the oldest continuous culture in the world. India, Meso-potamia, and Egypt were centers of high cultures earlier than China. But India suffered radical change because of the Indo-Aryan invasions of the second millennium B.C., and the ancient civilizations of Babylonia and Egypt have long since been overrun; they survive today only as they have contributed to succeeding civilizations. In this brief chapter, we are concerned only with the general background of the two indigenous schools of thought which arose in the classical feudal age of China; they have survived as Taoism and Confucianism.

The legendary history of China posits a series of dynasties, beginning in the Neolithic period. Although their precise nature is unclear, the listing of these dynasties serves to sketch in a sort of prehistory. There is the Hsia dynasty, traditionally dated from 2205 to 1766 B.C.; the Shang (eastern) dynasty, 1766-1122 B.C.; and finally, the great Chou dynasty, 1122-249 B.C. This last "Western" Dynasty predates the rule of any real emperor of China and was feudalistic in political and eco-nomic organization. Both Lao Tze and Confucius lived during the second half of this dynasty, 841-249 B.C. During this golden age of philosophy the enduring conservative bases of Chinese family life, government, and social organization were laid.

The religious practice of the early Chinese was that of typical early societies. It was a mixture of nature worship and reverence for ancestors. Both trends stressed a philosophy which made rhythm and harmony the goal of life. The worship of nature involved the conception of a sky-god called *T'ien,* and both the cosmic order of the planets, stars, and the sun and moon, and the orderly procession of the seasons were felt to set the true pattern for man's life. Birth, growth, and death were natural and orderly happenings, if one lived in harmony with the universe. Famine, storm, disease, war, and flood could all be traced to failure to live in harmony with the natural world. The cosmic order, *Li,* was natural and good; rulers and people should recognize this fact and live accordingly. The gods of nature were to be honored and placated in order to ensure safety, harmony, and prosperity.

At the same time, ancestor worship is found quite early, although this may have been mostly a cult of the aristocratic class. Many early societies appear to have taught that only the ruling classes have souls which can survive death, and it is probable that the Chinese, too, felt that the cult of ancestors was the special prerogative of the elite. In any case, reverence for the spirits of the departed was cultivated in order to insure prosperity and to avoid adverse influence from the powerful spirits of the dead. Ancestor worship also was thought to strengthen the continuity and harmony between living, departed, and yet unborn generations of men.

Two concepts important to later Chinese thought are found in this period. These are the notion of *Tao* (pronounced dhow) and of *yang* and *yin.* Tao, meaning the way, refers to the orderly movement of the natural world. Implicitly, it includes that mysterious, powerful, unrelenting force which causes the sun to rise and set, the rains to come, the crops to grow, and all the other forces of the natural world to operate.

Yang-yin is a more active expression of this same mysterious Tao; the double term refers to those active energies which inform and motivate existence. Yang represents the male principle and yin the female principle. The world and its beings and objects exist because of the interaction of these two principles. The famous Chinese symbol of a circle divided by an *S* into a light and a dark area expresses this concept. The yang male principle is the bright, active, warm, and by inference, the good aspect of the universe. The female yin is the principle of the dark, moist, cold, passive, and by inference, evil, aspect of existence. All things have their nature or character determined by dominance of one or the other principle. All men have in them, in varying amounts, some yin. All women, likewise, tend to vary in femininity, depending upon the yang in their nature. But, yang-yin is not confined to human beings, nor is it static. A tree which dies loses some yang force and becomes rotten, damp, and more yin.

Both Taoism and Confucianism describe the world in terms of yang-yin, and they also accept nature and ancestor worship. It is helpful, though an oversimplification, to say that each of these philosophies places its emphasis upon a different portion of the ancient Chinese tradition. Taoism builds upon the old way of nature worship, whereas Confucianism stresses the tradition of ancestor worship. Perhaps because the two differ principally in emphasis, they have been able to exist side by side with little conflict, over the centuries.

Chapter Fourteen

TAOISM

The religious philosophy known as *Taoism* (pronounced dhowism) presents nothing but problems to the historian who attempts to trace its beginnings. All religious movements desire to assert antiquity of origin, in order to claim timelessness for the truth they teach and to gain the accompanying authority. Legend ascribes the beginning of the Taoist movement to a shadowy figure called Lao Tzu, "the Old Master." Even his legendary dates are obscure, but he is supposed to have lived in the sixth century B.C., an older contemporary of Confucius. A basic document of Taoism, the *Tao Teh Ching,* is ascribed to Lao Tzu; the movement is supposed to have begun with it. Actually, the real Taoist school became well known only in the fourth century B.C. under the vigorous leadership of Chuang Tzu.

ORIGINS OF TAOISM

THE LEGEND OF LAO TZU. The earliest account of the life of Lao Tzu is the brief notice given him by Ssu-ma Ch'ien, a historian of the first century B.C. Details about Lao Tzu are sparse. According to legend, he was born about 604 B.C. and served as keeper of the royal archives. In his old age, becoming disgusted with the society of his day, he traveled to the west. Before Lao Tzu disappeared from the civilized world, a gatekeeper is reported to have asked him to write down his philosophy. This Lao Tzu did and then continued his journey into the wilds of central Asia.

THE TAO TEH CHING. The book which is ascribed to Lao Tzu is called by a Chinese title which means something like Way-Virtue-Classic, or "classic of the way of virtue." About 5,000 Chinese characters in length, it consists of eighty-one short poems on the meaning of Tao. The book is a prime source for modern attempts to recover the Taoist teachings. It contains no names of persons or places, and is almost impossible to date by internal evidence. Like the Fourth Gospel, its language and apparent meaning are simple, but on closer inspection are seen to be not only profound but capable of being interpreted variously. It is this possibility of interpretation at more than one level that has caused the book to be used as the basis for mystical speculations, which often lead in directions that probably would have amazed and confused the original author.

CHUANG TZU. In the fourth century B.C. this scholar composed a body of writings intended to introduce and explain the teachings of Taoism. By means of essays, stories, parables, and personal example, Chuang Tzu related Taoist philosophy to various aspects of the problems of existence. By studying the Tao Teh Ching, the writings of Chuang Tzu, and other fragmentary Taoist writings, it is possible to reconstruct, at least in outline, the probable teachings of the early Taoists.

THE WORLD VIEW OF TAOISM. Before we analyze Taoism in terms of our seven-point scheme, the concept of Tao as used in this philosophy requires comment. The word *Tao* literally means a "road" or "way." Here, however, it has the meaning of the natural way, the mysterious way of the universe. It would appear to be somewhat akin to the concept of a ground of being as taught in some mystical philosophies. The paramatman of Hinduism, for example, is self-existent, in need of no support or further cause. But Tao is immanent in a way that the paramatman is not; it is the very action of the universe in its natural course. The Tao cannot be defined but rather must be discerned. Tao can be discovered in the actions of all things that are allowed to proceed on their natural way, in the flight of a bird, the flow of a river, the rising of the sun, the change from autumn to winter. Tao sometimes is discerned in a negative manner when the natural way is blocked or actually opposed. To plough a field, to dam a river, to build a house, or to pass laws to govern men who should instead live by Tao, are all examples of going against Tao. Taoism holds that everything should be done according to Tao, the natural way; all else is madness and leads to disaster.

A corollary to the concept of Tao as the natural way is the often misunderstood teaching of *wu-wei,* or "not doing." Often interpreted as "passive," wu-wei affirms that the most effective way to live and act is to follow positively the natural way which in no fashion interferes with Tao. Wu-wei means "not acting" only in the sense that one does not himself try to influence the natural way, but merely follows Tao. A baby can cry all day and not become hoarse, a drunken person can fall out of a cart and not be hurt. Each "goes with Tao," does not resist or become tense, and thus does not suffer the consequences of such resistance to Tao.

The cosmos. Essentially, since it asserts that a single principle under-lies all that exists, Taoism is a monistic philosophy. Yang-yin, the male-female energy modes, are interpreted as aspects of the activity of Tao. The world of time and space, with its men, animals, and plants, is the ultimate expression of Tao.

The Way is like an empty vessel
That yet may be drawn from
Without ever needing to be filled.
*It is bottomless; the very progenitor of all things in the world.**

Deity. Since Taoism is monistic in principle, it contains no concept of deity in the sense of a creator or personal god. The universe exists naturally, by its own reflection of Tao. There is no god to pray to, since prayer cannot be answered by Tao. The universe in its cosmic actions follows Tao, and the world should do so too.

Man. Man also is an expression of Tao, a natural phenomenon that must find its place in the rhythmic order of nature. Man is not unlike animals, trees, and other things, animate and inanimate, since they, too, are expressions of this natural way. Were one to ask why it is that tigers kill and man thinks, the answer is that each is following his Tao: for one it is to kill; for the other, to think.

Man's plight. If man is but an expression of the Tao, why then is there evil in the world, why famine, war, disease, fear, and greed? Such undesirable things are caused by failure to know and to follow Tao. More than this, they are caused by active opposition to Tao, by flaunting the natural way, and by senseless attempts to improve upon nature. The Tao Teh Ching summarizes it (Chapter XXIX):

* Tao Teh Ching, IV, lines 1-4. Arthur Waley, trans., *The Way and Its Power: A Study of the Tao Tê Ching and Its Place in Chinese Thought* (London: George Allen & Unwin, Ltd.). Used by permission. A paperback edition is avail-able (New York: Grove Press, Inc., Evergreen Books, E84). Excerpts below are from the same translation.

Those that would gain what is under heaven by tampering with it—I
have seen that they do not succeed. For that which is under heaven is
like a holy vessel, dangerous to tamper with.
Those that tamper with it, harm it.
Those that grab at it, lose it.
For among the creatures of the world some go in front, some follow;
Some blow hot when others would be blowing cold.
Some are feeling vigorous just when others are worn out.
Some are loading just when others would be tilting out.
Therefore the Sage "discards the absolute, the all-inclusive, the extreme."

Salvation. What must man do to be saved in Taoism? The answer is
simple but profound. Follow Tao; learn its way and seek to conform to
it. Cease trying to remake nature and society into a humanly conceived
utopia. Such efforts are the source of strife and trouble. Follow wu-wei,
the natural way of non-doing. For non-doing is like water which drops
on a stone. The water follows its Tao, seeking its level, yet it wears
away the hardest stone. Animals live by Tao; they do not fight wars,
make slaves of other animals, or torture their enemies. Only man builds
economic and political systems and sets rules for society. Because of such
artificial systems there are greedy men, criminals, and tyrants. Accordingly, the Taoists condemn the Confucianists for teaching propriety, or
social morality, and urge men instead to go "back to nature." The Taoist
"golden age" to be recovered resembles the primitive way of life before
civilization.

But why do so few follow Tao, and so many follow instead the usual
ways of society? The answer lies in the monistic presupposition that all
things are an expression of the Tao. Just as the way of knowledge of the
Hindu Upanishads requires intuitive insight to realize "that thou art"—
knowledge which cannot be taught but must be induced by the teacher
and experienced by the student—the Way of Tao is to be apprehended
mystically, and then only by the few.

Conduct. If ethics is taken to mean a system of rules Taoism is opposed
to morality. The Tao Teh Ching (Chapter XIX) says:

Banish wisdom, discard knowledge,
And the people will be benefited a hundredfold.

Banish human kindness, discard morality,
And the people will be dutiful and compassionate.
Banish skill, discard profit,
And thieves and robbers will disappear.
If when these three things are done, they find life too plain and un-
* adorned,*
Then let them have accessories;
Give them Simplicity to look at, the Uncarved Block to hold,
Give them selflessness and fewness of desires.

If all men were to follow Tao and to refuse to try to improve upon
the natural way with man-made laws, all would be well. There would
be no theft if possessions were not valued; no adultery, if there were no
laws of marriage. Affirmatively, a "man of Tao" is gentle, not self-
seeking or greedy; he knows the way of heaven and follows it. Thus he
is "moral" without needing laws, and virtuous without having any rules
of virtue.

Destiny. Since man is an aspect of Tao, death is but another incident
in the eternal movements of nature. It is told of Chuang Tzu that he
sang and beat time on a wooden bowl, when his wife lay dead.
Reproached for this apparent callousness, he replied that her death was
but a change into a new aspect, as fall merges into winter, as a leaf drops
from a tree to become leaf mold. For him to grieve over her death would
be to show himself ignorant of Tao. In original Taoism, therefore, there
is no positive view of life after death, but only the idea of changing into
a new aspect of the monistic principle of Tao. And eventually that Tao
which brought order out of original chaos might permit the universe to
disintegrate again into its primordial state.

TAOISM THROUGH THE CENTURIES

TAOISM AS A POPULAR RELIGION. Even the writings of
Chuang Tzu never made Taoism popular as a philosophy. Its mysticism
and tendency to world renunciation did not appeal to the practical
Chinese. But in a perverse way, Taoism became the folk religion of
China. The teaching of Taoism that death presented no problems led
men to believe that the Taoist might know the secret of immortality and
that he might be able to control the world of spirits, good and bad, if

he truly understood the way of nature. Over the centuries, Taoism became a religion of superstition and of magical control of the processes of life, such as the fertility of animals, man, and the soil. The gods and goddesses of nature formed a Taoist pantheon, and Taoist priests became brewers of love potions, elixirs of immortality, and other magic drinks. A woman desiring to have a son would consult the Taoist priest, and a dutiful son seeking to protect his deceased father from evil spirits would seek an amulet or incantation from the same source.

THE ORGANIZATION OF TAOISM. Perhaps in competition with the Buddhists, who began to enter China just before the time of Christ, Taoism developed a monastic order. Legend has it that the Taoist leader, Chang Tao-Ling, first organized the Taoist priests in the second century A.D. He was known as the "Yellow Emperor," because his followers wore yellow turbans. The real center of monastic Taoism was Kiangsi Province in south central China.

Through the centuries, Taoism has had mixed fortunes. When in favor with the ruling dynasty, the leaders were sought out to aid the emperor by magical means, whether in waging war, securing male offspring, or preparing a drink to ensure immortality. But when Taoism was in disfavor, or if the wealth of the monasteries aroused the greed of outsiders, thousands of priests were put to the sword, often along with Buddhist monks who had similarly aroused the fury of the strong.

Because of the popular following enjoyed by Taoism, it has often had subterranean influences, difficult to measure. Secret societies with obvious Taoist leadership have existed well into the twentieth century. In 1848, the Taiping ("great peace") rebellion broke out against the Manchu dynasty and lasted until it was suppressed by "Chinese" Gordon in 1865. This revolution, which cost at least fifteen million lives, was religious in inspiration and undoubtedly strongly influenced by Taoist leadership. Today in China Taoism has no organization or independent existence, but undoubtedly continues in spirit among those superstitious practices of the farmers that survive Communist control.

TAOISM AND ZEN BUDDHISM. In recent years Taoism has received unexpected attention from Western intellectuals because of its formative influence on the Japanese school of Zen Buddhism. Zen ("meditation") is the Japanese equivalent of the Chinese *ch'an,* which in turn represents the Pali term, dhyana. Although Zen is atheistic it reflects the monism of Taoism as well. As opposed to the rational and intellectual philosophies of much of Mahayana Buddhism, Zen seeks to lead the inquirer, by means of meditation and physical exertion, to the point where he can relax, cease his mental striving and turmoil, and receive an intuitive awareness—*satori*—of the Void which is everything. In this awareness, as in Taoism, all human distinctions are blurred in the realization that everything is nothing, and nothing is all.

Many of the paradoxes of Taoism underlie Zen thought and practice. Judo, the art of self-defense, is the "soft way," just as ju-jitsu is the soft art, and the strong, self-assertive opponent defeats himself when he foolishly attacks a practitioner of judo. So too, Zen archery and swordsmanship apply the Taoist principle of wu-wei. Zen art, flower arrangement, and gardening reflect the return to the natural way as the beautiful and virtuous way. It is paradoxical that this anti-intellectual movement has become so attractive to intellectuals, but it also is true that many in the West have found in Zen a completely different and challenging approach to the meaning of existence.

Chapter Fifteen

CONFUCIANISM

The religion known as Confucianism traces its origins to the life and teachings of K'ung Fu Tzu. His family name was K'ung; Fu and Tzu are honorific titles meaning "revered master." The Latinized form of his name is Confucius. The Chinese name for the school of thought he founded is *Ju Chiao* (pronounced ru jow), which means "the School of the Scholars." For twenty-five hundred years, Confucianism has been the most influential movement in China, molding the educational, political, and social shape of Chinese culture. In addition to its role in determining the structure of Chinese society, it has also influenced greatly the cultures of Korea and Japan.

CLASSICAL CONFUCIANISM

THE LIFE OF CONFUCIUS. A great deal of information has been preserved concerning the life of Confucius. But certainly the tales we have are mixed with legendary material; the manuscript tradition of the sources is so tenuous that no clear agreement is to be found, especially between classical Confucian scholars and Western historians, on the accuracy of the texts. The traditional dates for Confucius are 551-479 B.C. This places him in the second part of the long Chou dynasty, that is, in the time before any true emperor had been able to unify China. It was a feudal age, characterized by the dominance of a hereditary nobility over a peasant or plebeian class. Constant wars, concomitant anarchy, and lack of stability in economic and family life were the rule.

Certain basic facts about Confucius' life are agreed upon and those germane to our purpose are here presented. He was probably a posthumous child, of the common people (legend gives him a hereditary rank, however), and raised in relative poverty by his mother. He received an education and was married at nineteen. Shortly after the birth of a son, he divorced his wife. Confucius earned his living, first as a menial laborer (again, legend has him found a school in his early twenties and earn his living by teaching), and later in different branches of government work. At about the age of fifty, he was appointed administrative ruler of his native state of Lu. This offered him an opportunity to apply his theories of government and to institute reforms in the province. He is reported to have resigned his post when the noble he served proved unable to resist the temptations of a gift of dancing girls and race horses, despite Confucius' teachings of virtue.

After this humiliating failure, Confucius spent ten years wandering through neighboring provinces, accompanied by several faithful disciples. He was searching for honest men and for rulers who desired good government. He was never offered a position which he considered worthy of him, and met with apathy and resistance. Finally, he returned to his home province and there established a school for pupils whom he felt to be ready for instruction.

The last decade of his life was spent on two important projects: the selection, editing, and use in his teaching of those ancient writings which he felt contained the true way of life for man and society and the development of a system of instruction which led to the establishment of the permanent school which survived him. At his death, Confucius is reported to have expressed the conviction that the world had ignored his efforts to reform society and to establish it upon sound principles. But history has proved otherwise.

THE CONFUCIAN SCRIPTURES. The Confucian scriptures have two main divisions: the first, the *Wu Ching,* or Five Classics, includes four early writings edited by Confucius, plus one ascribed to him; the second, the *Ssu Shu* (Four Books) is written about Confucius and his teachings by later Confucian scholars. Two problems associated with the recovery and translation of these writings are the discontinuity of the tradition—for the Emperor Shi-Huang-Ti (220-206 B.C.) ordered all Confucian bamboo books burned—and the obscurity of the ancient Chinese ideograms. This latter is most apparent when one compares any two English translations of these classics. In addition, it is probable that others besides Confucius had a hand in organizing the Five Classics into their present form.

The Wu Ching (Five Classics). The word translated "classic" is King or Ching (pronounced jing), which means "regular" or "canonical." Confucius is reported to have taken four ancient writings which he felt contained the best wisdom of the past, added a fifth, and made them available to his pupils.

THE SHU CHING (Book of History) contains ancient chronicles, court records, and traditions from the second millennium B.C. It is uninspiring reading, but contains much of value to the historian, especially since there are few other sources.

THE SHIH CHING (Book of Poetry) consists of over three hundred cultic and secular songs and odes. It affords some insight into early Chinese religion.

THE I CHING (Book of Changes) consists of a series of diagrams based on whole and broken lines, with commentary, not unlike, in intention, a modern horoscope.

THE LI-CHI (Book of Rites) contains cultic rites and court ceremonies.

THE CH'UN CH'IU (Spring and Autumn Annals) is supposed to have been written by Confucius himself, although this can scarcely be proved. The book is a chronicle of events in the province of Lu from 722 to 481 B.C., during the time of the Chou dynasty.

THE HSIAO CHING (Book of Filial Piety), a sixth classic, is sometimes included in this list. In the Confucian system of education, this short essay on the values of filial piety was the first work to be memorized by students.

The Ssu Shu (Four Books) are by Confucius' disciples and by later scholars.

THE LUN-YÜ, or Discourses of Confucius, consist of twenty books or chapters, mostly relating short anecdotes about Confucius. These are composed of questions asked by disciples and other persons, and his replies, as well as of stories telling how he acted in various situations. It is a prime source for his life and teachings.

THE TA HSUEH (Great Learning) is ascribed to a grandson of Confucius, Tzu Szu, and is a work on ethics and politics, expanding a chapter of the classic, the Li-Chi.

THE CHUNG YUNG (Central Harmony) also is ascribed to Tzu Szu, Confucius' grandson, and deals with the basis of moral law.

THE MENG TZE (Book of Mencius) is by the orthodox interpreter of Confucian thought who lived from 372-289 B.C. His writings include extensive traditions concerning Confucius and a clear elaboration of much of the latter's thought, especially on the theme of human nature.

BASIC CONFUCIAN PRINCIPLES. Before we analyze Confucian thought in terms of our seven-point scheme, several concepts basic to this religion must be noted. Of course, acceptance of Tao and of yang-yin are to be presupposed.

Filial piety. The belief in a hierarchy of all relationships is basic to Chinese thought. The son is inferior to his father and owes *hsiao*, respect and obedience, to him. So, too, the wife is inferior to her husband and owes him corresponding hsiao, the younger brother, servant, and citizen owe hsiao to elder brothers, master, and emperor.

Shu. These five relationships of hsiao, in which the inferior owes obedience to his superior, are matched by a reciprocal response called *shu* from the superior. The father, husband, older brother, master, and emperor properly reciprocate with condescension and with justice to those beneath them in station.

Shu is the basis of Confucius' maxim: "What you do not want done to yourself, do not do to others" (Lun Yü 15:23). Now, if an inferior-superior relationship is to be found in all areas of life, it appears that one may properly interpret this maxim of shu as do not do to those beneath you what you would not want those above you to do to you. Likewise, have proper hsiao or respect for those above you—do not treat others with a disrespect you would not want others to show to you.

Confucianism advocated classic virtues which are much like those of Greek Stoicism, but which must be described and given under their Chinese names.

JEN (pronounced run) has been translated as "benevolent love" and is the sum of virtues possible only for the mature and superior man; the boy or the inferior man is capable only of hsiao.

I (pronounced ee) is an ethical equivalent to duty; it describes the right behavior of a decent member of society.

CHIH (pronounced gee), means knowledge, wisdom, the insight or experience of the mature man.

HSIN (shin) means truth, sincerity; its stress on integrity redeems Confucianism from the charge of exaggerated formalism.

LI, politeness, propriety, has the outward aspect of face saving, and of always acting like a true gentleman. It also, however, has to do with that force of inner character which includes the whole man.

The Chün Tze. This term (pronounced jewin dzu) is given a special meaning by Confucius: it means "sons of the princes," or nobility. Instead of approving of the concept of hereditary nobility, Confucius taught that the true gentleman or nobleman was such because of character. The chün tze, accordingly, is the Confucian ideal. Armed with the belief that, endowed by heaven, all men are born good, Confucius sought to create a true nobility by proper education and by the inculcation, in their proper order and balance, of all the virtues.

The four classes. The feudal stratification of life in China is the implicit base of much Confucian thought. For, in the feudal scale, the lowest social rank is that of the merchant, who trades what others produce. Next in the scale is the artisan, who makes things out of what the farmer grows. Higher still comes the farmer, who produces the necessities of physical life. And highest is the scholar, who alone can become the chün tze. As a corollary, the soldier is a social outcast, for he destroys what others produce. Into this social stratification Confucius introduced the leavening dictum that anyone can become a scholar and rise in social rank. To this day, the scholar stands first in rank in the Confucian hierarchy.

THE WORLD VIEW OF CONFUCIANISM.

Although many hold that Confucianism is not a religion, but merely a system of political and social thought, it seems to have all the basic qualities of a true religion. The following analysis makes no attempt to differentiate between what Confucius himself may have taught and later developments, but the emphasis is upon a statement of early Confucian thought.

The cosmos. Confucius referred to himself as a transmitter of the best of the past; he denied being an innovator. He used such terms as Tao and yang-yin and held the traditional view that the universe consisted of heaven, the earth, and the "ten thousand things," i.e., the world of men, animals, and plants. The overarching sky represented the "way of heaven," and was good and natural.

Deity. Confucius held a more personal conception of the way of nature (Tao) than that taught by Taoism. Two terms for a sort of natural deity appear in the *Analects*. One is the term *Shang-Ti* (used but once in the Analects, though employed in later Confucian thought) which means something like "exalted ancestor" and might refer to a sky-god of ancient origin. The term *T'ien,* which means sky, or heaven, is used much more frequently. Confucius said that heaven supported his work and that it was necessary for the chün tze to know the ways of heaven. He also believed in prayer to heaven.

In relation to popular nature and ancestor worship, Confucius appears to have been primarily agnostic. He never opposed belief in, or appeasement of, spirits of nature; it is probable that, in this respect, he simply accepted the customs of his day.

Man. Man needs only to realize his natural goodness endowed by heaven. This requires education and inculcation of the virtues. The hope of developing the chün tze in an ideal society discloses the humanistic character of Confucian thought. Yet a class society is assumed; man is superior to woman, and the virtues of hsiao and shu assume the superior-inferior relationships of feudalism.

Man's plight. Confucius believed that he lived in a day when the ancient ways were ignored; proper relationships between classes and the sexes were upset; and heaven, earth, and the ways of men were out of harmony. Such a state was caused by men's failure to follow the proper way of the ancients; because of this failure disasters—war, famine, and human degradation—threatened to destroy culture and society.

Salvation. The answer to man's need was simple: return to the way of the ancestors. Study the classics to discover the ancient way of virtue. Instead of thinking that nobility is a matter of birth, realize that it is a moral achievement, open to all, though attained by few. For Confucius, the golden age lay in the past and his concern was to recreate it. But whereas the Taoist wanted to restore the simple way of the world of nature before civilization corrupted it, Confucius wanted to return to an idealized age of ancient heroes, such as the legendary emperors, Yao, Shun, and Yü.

Conduct. The right way to act is to follow the way of the ancients. The ideal of chün tze pertained to the man who always knew what was right and followed his knowledge. The ideal is based, however, upon the assumption that the "five relationships," with their accompanying virtues of hsiao and shu, are true teachings and should be followed. Beyond this, it was held that injury is to be treated with justice, as is proper in the ideal society, and kindness is to be repaid with kindness, as is fitting. Li, or propriety, is the guide to right conduct, and the action of a gentleman is the norm. In this respect there is some disagreement among historians concerning Confucius himself. The tenth chapter of the Analects describes in elaborate detail the conduct of a gentleman, including such details as the proper color of his clothes, but it is probable that this is an idealized picture of a noble courtier, although the preserved text makes the descriptions refer to Confucius himself.

Destiny. When Confucius was asked about death, he replied: "Why do you ask me about death when you do not know how to live?" Here, as in relation to the concept of deity, Confucius was an agnostic. Nevertheless, he did not oppose the traditional view, and throughout its history, Confucianism has stressed heavily the cult of ancestors. Accordingly, it is proper to revere the memory of the ancestors and to think in terms of some sort of survival of a spirit after death. In this connection, we find much emphasis upon the need to have sons who will honor the father as an ancestor. So again, even in relation to destiny, Confucius turned men's thoughts, not to the future, but to the past, to the way of the ancestors.

CONFUCIANISM IN HISTORY

How can we account for the dramatic success of the teachings of Confucius—for the fact that it is the most powerful single influence upon the culture and history of China? First, it should be noted that Confucius made available, in his Classics, a curriculum for the education of the boys of China. His educational system was developed in subsequent centuries, until it became the normal method of teaching. But the truly radical contribution of Confucius, which served as a leavening and even revolutionary factor in Chinese society, was his teaching that the chün tze, the true nobility, were men of character rather than birth. Perhaps Confucius lived just at a time when writing and education were beginning to become easily available to those who could afford to learn, and his contributions therefore assumed great importance. In any event, what purports to be his teachings have proved to be normative through the 2,500 years since he lived.

THE "SCHOOL OF THE SCHOLAR." The first true emperor of China, Shi-Huang-Ti (221-207 B.C.), who headed the spartan Ch'in dynasty, attempted to eradicate Confucian teachings from his realm, probably because they represented too fully the conservative past and were opposed to his revolutionary reforms. But his order to burn all the Confucian books was not successful in destroying this philosophy. The assiduous scholars who survived Shi-Huang-Ti's short-lived regime were able to reconstruct the texts from memory, and also probably from salvaged books. Having survived this disaster, thenceforth Confucianism thrived. Before this time, the writings and influence of the great Mencius (372-289 B.C.) and his younger contemporary, Hsün Tze (318-235

B.C.), had helped to stabilize the teachings of the Confucian philosophy and to broaden its appeal.

Although the several centuries after Confucius are known as the "period of the one hundred schools," only the two main schools of thought which we have treated, Taoism and Confucianism, survived. By the first century A.D., the third traditional Chinese school or doctrine, Buddhism, had been introduced from India. Confucianism became known in this context as Ju Chiao, or the School of the Scholar. The most significant development of Confucian thought since that time took place during the Sung dynasty, when neo-Confucianism arose as a philosophical system. This was primarily an attempt to develop a metaphysic in competition with that of Mahayana Buddhism. The most important neo-Confucianist was Chu Hsi (1130-1200 A.D.). This school taught that two principles, spirit and law, produce all things. With the dualistic position that ch'ih (spirit) and li (law) explain all things, neo-Confucian thought resisted the monistic tendencies of both Taoism and Buddhism.

CONFUCIANISM'S POLITICAL AND SOCIAL INFLU-ENCE. It is ironical that the revolutionary tenet of Confucius—that nobility results not from birth but from character—and the attempts of the first real emperor to destroy Confucianism as a threat to his rule were followed in later centuries by ruling dynasties, frequently using Confucianism for their support. Although Confucius also taught that the ruler must follow the way of heaven and treat his subjects with kindness and justice, this was disregarded and the emphasis upon filial piety and loyalty to the way of the ancestors became dominant. The person of the emperor gained prestige in connection with his role in the state cult of Confucianism; in it, the emperor annually, at the winter solstice, sacrificed to the gods of nature and to the ancestors on the gigantic altar south of Peking, in order to insure the peace and prosperity of the nation.

Confucianism also placed great importance upon the family. A man must have sons in order to be worshiped as an ancestor. This has often led to the taking of concubines when the first marriage proved either to be fruitless or to produce only girls. Not only were the sons required to be obedient to the father and the family, but the family was projected into the past, by means of ancestor worship, and into the future, by the desire of sons to continue their own immortality by having male offspring. The local Confucian temple became primarily a place where one went to report to one's ancestors on problems and decisions of the living family. The ancestors were represented by stone tablets bearing the names of the departed. As time passed, the older stones were moved outside and piled up, and the more recent tablets were given central place. With stress upon a loyal son's burying his ancestors, the Confucian temples and graveyards became prominent features of the Chinese village and reminders of the duty of reverence for the past and for the ways of the ancients.

MODERN DEVELOPMENTS. After the revolution of 1911, which overthrew the Manchu dynasty, President Sun Yat Sen, attempting reform, used the prestige of Confucianism in various ways. Nevertheless, Western education, science, and Marxist teachings continued to erode the ancient way of Confucius. Then, in 1949, the Communist rule of Mao Tse-tung took over. Today, the government officially opposes both Confucianism's stress on loyalty to the family rather than the central government, and its teaching that the ancient ways are best. Mao Tse-tung and others have called upon the Chinese to look to the future for their true salvation and to root out all that is old or traditional. Although old ways die slowly, especially in an agrarian culture, there is no doubt that the future of Confucianism is dim.

Chapter Sixteen

SHINTO

Shinto is the indigenous religion of Japan; although it has been influenced by Chinese thought and practice and, via Buddhism, by the religious thought of India, Shinto today still is close to the primitive attitude toward the world which is found in its early scriptures. Since most Japanese not only follow Shinto ways of thinking and acting, but also Buddhist and Confucian practices, it is somewhat artificial to offer a construct of Shinto and to suggest that this is truly what a follower of this religion thinks and does. So, too, a German Nazi, who claimed to follow the Norse gods and practice the ways of a "superman," might also have kept much that was Christian in his thoughts and deeds. The following analysis is therefore artificial and is intended merely to introduce the reader to the meaning of Shinto.

CLASSICAL SHINTO

THE ORIGINS OF JAPAN. The aboriginal inhabitants of Japan, known mostly through legend, were a race of short people. Later the Ainu came to the Japanese islands from the mainland; they are still found today on the northern island of Sakhalin. They are noted for their hairy appearance and, like the American Indian, live mostly on government reservations. Two later groups of invaders complete the amalgam which is the Japanese people: mainland group of northern Mongols from Korea and a southern group of Malayan stock from south China and the islands of the South Pacific.

The term *Shinto* is composed of the Chinese words *shen* and *tao*, which mean spirit and way. The Japanese equivalent is *kami no michi*, *kami* meaning spirit or god, *no* being the possessive particle, and *michi* meaning way. There is no final agreement among either Japanese or Western scholars upon the meaning of kami, the key concept in this religion. Some would have kami mean something like mana, the Melanesian word found throughout the Pacific islands. This would give the concept of kami the force of the primitive concept of supernatural amoral power. Much of Shinto belief would appear to fit this interpretation. Another definition of kami would have it mean high, or upper. One problem connected with the clarification of Japanese terms is that there is little help from cognate or parallel languages, like that available when defining Sanskrit or Hebrew terms. Kami does carry the connotation of awesomeness and holiness, and since it is a synonym for god or spirit, it obviously has a range of meaning which cannot be embraced in one word.

SHINTO SCRIPTURES. According to tradition, Buddhism entered Japan from the mainland in 522 A.D. This foreign religion eventually stimulated concern to preserve the indigenous religion of Shinto, and in the eighth century the oral myths and traditions were recorded in two documents. The first of these, dated 712 A.D., is the *Kojiki* (Records of Ancient Matters). It is written in Chinese characters, which complicates translation. It contains cosmogonic myths, genealogies of the gods, and records of the reigns of early emperors. The second, dated 720 A.D., is the *Nihongi,* also called *Nihon Shoki* (Chronicles of Japan), and includes materials omitted in the Kojiki, bringing the records down to the time of its writing. Both scriptures fall into the category of myth and legend rather than history, and are the primary documents of Shinto. A later writing, the *Yengishiki* (Institutes of the Period of Yengi), is from the tenth century and contains information about the official cult. This document also includes examples of the *norito,* prayers used to supplicate the deities.

THE SHINTO WORLD VIEW. A reconstruction of the world view of classical Shinto is necessarily artificial for several reasons. In the first place, the very writing down of the sacred writings in the eighth century was arbitrary, resulting from imperial decree, rather than spontaneous growth. Again, Shinto as practiced then and now is basically a folk religion of nature and ancestor worship, so that the official Japanese description of its relation to the imperial dynasty represents only one aspect of its meaning in the life of the people. And, most important, Chinese and Buddhist elements have so influenced the indigenous religion that all attempts to recover a pure Shinto necessarily are speculative and arbitrary. With these caveats, the following analysis is presented.

The cosmos. The myth of creation in the Kojiki tells of a cosmic egg dividing to form heaven and earth. This myth reflects the yang-yin of Chinese thought. The purer or positive portion of the egg-shaped mass ascended to form the sky, and the grosser, negative portion descended to form the earth and sea. From this beginning, in time different deities appeared, and finally a male and female couple, Izanagi and Izanami. These mated and produced the sacred Japanese islands and other deities. Accordingly, the Japanese islands are believed to be the center of the earth and of divine origin, as were their first inhabitants who later sprang from the gods.

Deity. The basic concept of deity in Shinto is the concept of kami. Kami seems to describe anything holy, unusual, or connected with the world of the spirit. The universe is populated with "eight hundred myriads of kami beings." Amaterasu, the sun-goddess; Tsuki-yomi, the moon-god; and Susa-no-wo, the storm-god have roles of central importance, and their origins are described in the myths. It is interesting to note that, contrary to the usual primitive myth, the sun is feminine, the moon masculine. The storm-god represents the capricious and destructive forces of nature working against the benign rule of the sun-goddess. In addition, outstanding natural objects, such as Mount Fujiyama and the Japanese islands themselves, are regarded as kami beings.

In addition to nature deities, the ancestors constitute an important part of the Shinto pantheon. The sun-goddess, Amaterasu, had a divine grandson, Jimmu Tenno, who descended to the sacred islands to rule the Japanese people. His rule, according to tradition, began in 660 B.C., and the imperial line he founded has remained unbroken to this day. In fact there is no historical basis for this claim, but the Imperial Rescript on Education, published in 1890, required that all children be taught the divinity of the emperor and his direct descent from the sun-goddess. Actually, the intent of this teaching is to inculcate the belief that the great heroes of Japanese history, as well as members of the royal line, partake so much of kami power that they are truly divine. We find, then, that the kami concept can be understood as involving both nature and ancestor worship.

Man. Shinto teaches that all living beings are possessed of kami nature. A fox or a cat has kami power in it. But man is of a higher level because of greater kami force in him. In this sense, man is conceived as divine or spirit-possessed. Man, then, has two aspects, his bodily part and his kami nature, which he is to nourish and keep pure. But even here there are degrees of kami possession, man being superior to woman, while the emperor is superior to all humans because he is a direct descendant of the kami being, Amaterasu. Before Japan's defeat in World War II, the emperor's person was at most times protected from even the gaze of profane or ordinary persons, and no one was ever permitted to look down upon him from a roof or other high place.

Man's plight. There are two main causes of trouble and evil in the world. The first has to do with actions which might unleash dangerous kami potency. Again, the Shinto myths tell of certain polluting actions of Susa-no-wo which caused distress to his sister, Amaterasu; he broke down dikes between rice fields; he deposited excrement beneath her throne. Such myths symbolize the nature of polluting actions and stress the need to avoid them. But any violation of the many tabus, such as hanging a boy's clothes on a hook intended for girl's clothes or contact with a polluting agency such as blood, can cause misfortune.

The second source of misfortune is the displeasure of ancestors or of the gods. If they are neglected—not informed of activities of the family or nation or not propitiated with offerings of food and wine—they may become displeased; then trouble will ensue. Even more important as a cause of misfortune is disloyalty to the gods or the emperor, or any failure on the part of the individual to measure up to his highest capacity in relation to his family or nation. This is a heightened aspect of the primitive emphasis upon group loyalty for the purpose of insuring the welfare of the tribe. And it represents the extreme of the Confucian teaching of hsiao or filial piety in that complete obedience to the emperor is taught as the duty of every citizen, a duty whose nonfulfillment will be disastrous.

Salvation. Salvation is to be found, first of all, in observing all tabus and avoiding persons and objects which might cause pollution. The gods and goddesses of agriculture are propitiated by offerings, prayers, and ceremonies, including two annual national ceremonies of purification in which the emperor acts on behalf of the nation. Fetishes also are employed, for example, a phallic-shaped pole may be placed in the center of a path leading to a bridge. That pole has the power to hold back demons who might seek to follow a person onto the bridge and hurl him into the water.

But the most important law of salvation calls for obedience to the emperor as a kami being. If all obey the emperor and work for the common good of the Japanese nation, then the whole world of nature and of men will be in harmony, and peace and prosperity will prevail.

The famous ritualistic suicide known as *hara-kari* is practiced by a loyal subject who fails in his duty. Even if failure is in no way his fault, by this ultimate sacrifice the Shinto believer demonstrates his loyalty and sincerity and, incidentally, guarantees himself immortality among the ancestral kami beings.

Conduct. Kami power in itself is amoral; it is simply force possessing no qualities of good or evil. It therefore is dangerous rather than malicious. Man as a being possessed with kami has no god to obey, but needs only to know how to adjust to kami in its various manifestations. Shinto thus lacks an ethical system. Or rather, if one truly expresses his kami nature and follows the tabus and rules of society, he is doing right.

Into Shinto were introduced specific ethical teachings from two sources. The first was the Confucian ethic from China. The five relationships of life and the requirement of filial piety were adopted, but the Japanese emphasis omitted the element of Shu or reciprocity. Obedience to one's superior was taught, but little if anything was said about justice and kindness as the correct response to obedience. The other contribution to ethics was *Bushido,* the cavalier ethic associated with Buddhism. Yet this vaunted code was for the fighting knights, or samurai, and was not necessarily applicable to the commoner. Good conduct under Shinto, therefore, basically requires a man to fit into the group pattern and to express his kami nature.

Destiny. Shinto teaches a cult of ancestors which is like certain Confucian teachings, but is probably of independent origin rather than the result of borrowing. Since one's kami nature will survive death, a man desires to be worthy of being remembered with approbation by his descendants. Therefore it is preferable to die than to fail in duty to one's family or nation. The famous *kamikaze* pilots of World War II acted on this principle. Kamikaze means "divine wind," and refers to a providential storm which destroyed the Chinese invasion fleet of Kublai Khan off the coast of Japan in the thirteenth century. A kamikaze pilot, by his brave but suicidal action in the national cause, exemplified the height of loyalty to the emperor and his people. He then became an illustrious ancestor, joining the eight hundred myriads of kami beings in the spirit world.

From Mahayana Buddhism was borrowed, as part of Japanese thinking about death, the teaching of eternal life and also of the more specific concepts of a heaven and a hell as abodes after death.

SHINTO IN JAPANESE HISTORY

SHINTO AND BUDDHISM. The Buddhism that entered Japan in the sixth century A.D. was of the tolerant Mahayana form. It had already developed a pattern of adaptation in its movement through China where it adopted gods and goddesses—the goddess of mercy, Kwan Yin, for example—as Bodhisattvas. Shinto had not given rise to much philosophical speculation or teaching about man's destiny. Buddhism, without attempting to reform or alter the ancient ways, tended to fill many gaps in the religious life of the Japanese. The Mahayana teaching of "the Buddha in every man," and the monistic tendency to consider various gods of nature and ancestors as embodiments of the Buddha, helped Buddhism to adapt optimally to the new locale. When in later centuries some opposition to Buddhism arose in the name of Japanese nationalism, the foreign religion had become so well entrenched that it could not be driven out.

One cult arising from the mingling of Buddhism and Shinto identified the two religions as aspects of each other, and came to be known as *Ryobu,* or Dual, *Shinto.*

Sect Shinto refers to the folk religion practiced by millions of Japanese. There are thirteen main sects with temples, priests, and schools, and they represent a strong conservative tradition in Japanese culture.

Shrine Shinto is also called *State Shinto* and was a key factor in the Meiji reform. (From 1603 to 1868, the Tokugawa regime had isolated Japan from all outside influences.) During the Meiji regime after 1868, Shinto was strengthened and reformed at the expense of Buddhism; certain important Shinto shrines were placed under government control and the national cultic practices of Shinto were given new prominence. Although the official position of the Japanese government, as represented to the West, was that such ceremonies and shrines were little different from a Veteran's Day service at Arlington National Cemetery in Virginia, they were actually utilized by the Japanese leaders to further religious patriotism. After World War II, General MacArthur ordered the disestablishment of Shrine (State) Shinto, and today it has no financial support from the government.

AFTER WORLD WAR II. Japanese military leaders used Shinto as vigorously as possible to encourage their people to a total war effort between 1941 and 1945. The crushing defeat suffered by Japan was unbelievable to many Shintoists. Many even began to turn to Christianity, believing it to be the more potent religion, because it had led the Allies to victory. More recently there has been a readjustment; not only is Buddhism evidencing new vitality and leadership, making Japan the real center of Mahayana Buddhism, but neo-Shintoism has many followers. This movement is not dissimilar to German Nazism in its narrow nationalism and emphasis upon a sacred soil and people. It does not, however, appear to have much future in the face of other movements, such as socialism, communism, and materialism of the sort to be found in present-day Europe and America. Since Shinto is basically a nature religion, its strength and influence will continue in inverse ratio to the increasing urbanization and scientific education of the people.

A BIBLIOGRAPHY OF PAPERBOUND BOOKS

ON THE WORLD'S RELIGIONS

The following bibliography approximately follows the outline of this book, except that books dealing with all or most of the world's religions are listed first, followed by bibliographies for each of the sixteen chapters. Each list is divided into primary sources—translations of scriptures and classical authors—and secondary writings about the religion.

The quality of paperbound books on religion is excellent, and the number is rapidly expanding. It now is possible to teach even advanced courses in the history of religions using only paperbacks. The following lists include some duplication of titles when several presses offer the same books. For Christianity and Judaism, due to limitations of space, there are many omissions. For three religions, Zoroastrianism, Jainism, and Sikhism, no scriptures or monographs are available, and there are no books dealing specifically with Shinto. A short list of general treatments of religions which include chapters on these four faiths is therefore part of this bibliography.

The sources for this bibliography are varied, including publishers' catalogues, several cumulative lists of paperbacks, and *The New York Times* and *New York Herald Tribune* book review supplements devoted to paperbacks. The R. R. Bowker Company, 62 West 45th Street, New York 36, publishes a quarterly (in paperback), *Paperbound Books in Print,* available for a nominal price. Although it was necessary to exclude paperbacks published in foreign countries, Mr. Basil Blackwell of Blackwell's, Broad Street, Oxford, England, has announced the availability through his company of a catalogue of English paperbacks on all subjects.

ANTHOLOGIES OF SCRIPTURES

Ballou, Robert O., ed., *The Portable World Bible*. New York: The Viking Press, Inc., Viking Paperbound Portables, P5.

Bouquet, A. C., *Sacred Books of the World*. Baltimore: Penguin Books, Inc., A283.

Browne, Lewis, *The World's Great Scriptures*. New York: The Macmillan Company, Macmillan Paperbacks, 54.

Champion, Selwyn Gurney and Dorothy Short, *Readings from World Religions*. New York: Fawcett Publications, Inc., Premier Books, D85.

Gaer, Joseph, *Wisdom of the Living Religions*. New York: Apollo Editions, Inc., A24.

Yohannan, John D., ed., *A Treasury of Asian Literature*. New York: New American Library of World Literature, Inc., Mentor Books, MT340.

ON THE WORLD'S RELIGIONS

Allen, E. L., *Christianity Among the Religions*. Boston: Beacon Press, LR9.

Berry, Gerald L., *The Religions of the World*. New York: Barnes & Noble, Everyday Handbooks, 224.

Bouquet, A. C., *Comparative Religion*. Baltimore: Penguin Books, Inc., A89.

Braden, Charles S., *The World's Religions,* rev. Nashville, Tenn.: Abingdon Press, Apex Books, C1.

Browne, Lewis, *This Believing World*. New York: The Macmillan Company, MP83.

Ceadel, Eric B., ed., *Literatures of the East: A Survey*. New York: Grove Press, Inc., Evergreen Books, E167.

Cogley, John, gen. ed., *Religion in America*. Cleveland: The World Publishing Company, Meridian Books, M60.

Danielou, Jean, *The Salvation of the Nations*. Notre Dame, Ind.: University of Notre Dame Press, NDP-12.

Gaer, Joseph, *How the Great Religions Began,* rev. ed. New York: New American Library of World Literature, Inc., Signet Key Books, KD359.

James, Edwin Oliver, *Comparative Religion*. New York: Barnes and Noble, 1961.

Kitagawa, Joseph M., ed., *Modern Trends in World Religions*. La Salle, Ill.: The Open Court Publishing Co., P81.

Kramer, Samuel Noah, *Mythologies of the Ancient World*. New York: Doubleday & Company, Inc., Anchor Books, A229.

Landis, Benson Y., *World Religions*. New York: E. P. Dutton & Co., Inc., Dutton Everyman Paperbacks, D48.

Lewis, John, *Religions of the World Made Simple*. Garden City, N.Y.: Doubleday & Company, Inc., Made Simple Books, MS27.

Northrop, F. S. C., *The Meeting of East and West*. New York: The Macmillan Co., 8.

Parrinder, E. G., *Introduction to Asian Religions*. Greenwich, Conn.: Seabury Press, Seraph Books.

Pike, E. Royston, *Encyclopaedia of Religion and Religions*. Cleveland: The World Publishing Company, Meridian Books, MG37.

Potter, Charles Francis, *Faiths Men Live By*. New York: Ace Books and Ace Star Books, K101.

————, *Great Religious Leaders*. New York: Washington Square Press, Inc., W1077.

Radhakrishnan, S., *Eastern Religions and Western Thought*. New York: Oxford University Press, Inc., Galaxy Books, 27.

Ross, Floyd H. and Tynette Hills, *The Great Religions by Which Men Live. (Questions That Matter Most Asked by the World's Great Religions)*. New York: Fawcett Publications, Inc., Premier Books, D120.

Rosten, Leo, ed., *A Guide to the Religions of America*. New York: Simon & Schuster, Inc., 6141.

Smith, Huston, *The Religions of Man*. New York: New American Library of World Literature, Inc., Mentor Books, MT350.

Wach, Joachim, *The Comparative Study of Religions*, Joseph M. Kitagawa, ed. New York: Columbia University Press, 28.

Zaehner, R. C., *The Comparison of Religions*. Boston: Beacon Press, LR15.

Chapter One: Man and Religion

Bulfinch, Thomas, *Bulfinch's Mythology*, abr. by Edmund Fuller. New York: Dell Publishing Company, Inc., Dell Books.

Campbell, Joseph, *The Hero with a Thousand Faces*. Cleveland: The World Publishing Company, Meridian Books, M22.

Cassirer, Ernst, *Language and Myth*, trans. Suzanne K. Langer. New York: Dover Publications, Inc.

Du Nouy, Lecomte, *Human Destiny*. New York: New American Library of World Literature, Inc., Mentor Books, MP410.

Eliade, Mircea, *Cosmos and History: The Myth of the Eternal Return*. New York: Harper & Brothers, Harper Torchbooks, TB50.

————, *The Sacred and the Profane*. New York: Harper & Brothers, Harper Torchbooks, TB81.

Ferm, V., *Encyclopedia of Religion*. Paterson, N.J.: Littlefield, Adams and Company, 139.

Frazer, James, *The Golden Bough*, abr. New York: The Macmillan Company, 5.

Freud, Sigmund, *The Future of an Illusion*. New York: Doubleday & Company, Inc., Anchor Books, A99.

————, *Basic Writings: Totem and Taboo*. New York: Modern Library, G39.

Gaster, Theodor H., *Thespis*. New York: Doubleday & Company, Inc., Anchor Books, A230.

Heiler, Friedrich, *Prayer: A Study in the History and Psychology of Religion*, trans. and ed. by Samuel McComb. New York: Oxford University Press, Inc., Galaxy Books, 16.

James, William, *The Varieties of Religious Experience*. New York: The New American Library of World Literature, Inc., Mentor Books, MT320.

Jung, C. G., *Psyche and Symbol,* Violet S. de Laszlo, ed. New York: Doubleday & Company, Inc., Anchor Books, A136.

———, *Psychology and Religion.* New Haven, Conn.: Yale University Press, Y14.

La Barre, Weston, *The Human Animal.* Chicago: University of Chicago Press, Phoenix Books, P45.

Langer, Susanne K., *Philosophy in a New Key.* New York: New American Library of World Literature, Inc., Mentor Books, MD101.

Otto, Rudolf, *The Idea of the Holy.* New York: Oxford University Press, Inc., Galaxy Books, 114.

———, *Mysticism East and West.* Cleveland: The World Publishing Company, Meridian Books, Inc., LA14.

Rank, Otto, *The Myth of the Birth of the Hero and Other Essays.* New York: Alfred A. Knopf, Inc., Vintage Books, Inc., V10.

Robinson, Herbert S. and Knox Wilson, *Myths and Legends of All Nations.* New York: Bantam Books, Inc., FR10.

Simmel, Georg, *Sociology of Religion.* New York: Philosophical Library, Inc., Wisdom Library Paperbacks.

Smith, Homer, *Man and His Gods.* New York: Grosset & Dunlap, Inc., Universal Library, 5.

Stace, W. T., *The Teachings of the Mystics.* New York: New American Library of World Literature, Inc., Mentor Books, MD306.

Thouless, R. H., *Introduction to the Psychology of Religion.* New York: Cambridge University Press, 1961.

Underhill, Evelyn, *The Golden Sequence: A Fourfold Study of the Spiritual Life.* New York: Harper & Brothers, Harper Torchbooks, TB68.

———, *Mysticism.* Cleveland: The World Publishing Company, Meridian Books, MG1.

Wach, Joachim, *Sociology of Religion* (reissue). Chicago: University of Chicago Press, Phoenix Books, P92.

Zaehner, R. C., *Mysticism Sacred and Profane: An Inquiry into Some Varieties of Praeternatural Experience.* New York: Oxford University Press, Inc., Galaxy Books, 56.

Zilboorg, Gregory, *Freud and Religion.* Westminster, Md.: The Newman Press, 1961.

Zimmer, Heinrich, *The King and the Corpse,* ed. by Joseph Campbell. Cleveland: The World Publishing Company, Meridian Books, M93.

CHAPTER TWO: THE RELIGION OF PRIMITIVE PEOPLES

Leslie, Charles, ed., *Anthropology of Folk Religion.* New York: Random House, Vintage Books, Inc., V105.

Lowie, Robert H., *Primitive Religion.* New York: Grosset & Dunlap, Inc., Universal Library, 35.

———, *Primitive Society.* New York: Harper & Brothers, Harper Torchbooks, TB1056.

Malinowski, Bronislaw, *Magic, Science and Religion and Other Essays.* New York: Doubleday & Company, Inc., Anchor Books, A23.

Nida, Eugene A. and William A. Smalley, *Introducing Animism.* New York: Friendship Press, no. 108.

Radin, Paul, *Primitive Man as Philosopher.* New York: Dover Publications, Inc., T392.

———, *Primitive Religion.* New York: Dover Publications, Inc., T393.

———, *The World of Primitive Man.* New York: Grove Press, Inc., Evergreen Books, E214.

Slotkin, James S., *The Peyote Religion: A Study in Indian-White Relations.* New York: Free Press of Glencoe, 1956.

Sumner, William Graham, *Folkways.* New York: Dover Publications, Inc.

———, *Folkways.* New York: New American Library of World Literature, Inc., Mentor Books, MT297.

Tylor, Edward B., *Anthropology,* abr. Ann Arbor, Mich.: University of Michigan Press, Ann Arbor Paperbacks, 44.

———, *Origins of Culture* (Part 1 of *Primitive Culture*). New York: Harper & Brothers, Harper Torchbooks, TB-33.

———, *Religion in Primitive Culture* (Part 2 of *Primitive Culture*). New York: Harper & Brothers, Harper Torchbooks, TB-34.

CHAPTER THREE: THE ANCIENT NEAR EAST

SCRIPTURES

Gaster, Theodor H., *The Oldest Stories in the World.* Boston: Beacon Press, BP66.

Grant, Frederick C., ed., *Ancient Roman Religion.* Indianapolis, Ind.: The Liberal Arts Press Division of The Bobbs-Merrill Company, Inc., Library of Liberal Arts, LLA138.

———, *Hellenistic Religions: The Age of Syncretism.* Indianapolis, Ind.: The Liberal Arts Press Division of The Bobbs-Merrill Company, Inc., Library of Liberal Arts, LLA134.

Mendelsohn, Isaac, ed., *Religions of the Ancient Near East: Sumero-Akkadian Religious Texts and Ugaritic Epics.* Indianapolis, Ind.: The Liberal Arts Press Division of The Bobbs-Merrill Company, Inc., Library of Liberal Arts, LLA136.

THE ANCIENT NEAR EAST AND THE
GREEK AND ROMAN WORLDS

Albright, W. F., *Archaeology of Palestine.* Baltimore: Penguin Books, Inc., A199.

———, *From the Stone Age to Christianity,* 2nd ed. New York: Doubleday & Company, Inc., Anchor Books, A100.

Breasted, James Henry, *Development of Religion and Thought in Ancient Egypt.* New York: Harper & Brothers, Harper Torchbooks, TB57.

Burrows, Millar, *What Mean These Stones?* Cleveland: The World Publishing Company, Meridian Books, LA7.

Chiera, Edward, *They Wrote on Clay,* ed. George G. Cameron. Chicago: University of Chicago Press, Phoenix Books, P2.

Childe, V. Gordon, *New Light on the Most Ancient East.* New York: Grove Press, Inc., Evergreen Books, E72.

Cumont, Franz, *After Life in Roman Paganism.* New York: Dover Publications, Inc., 1960.

——, *Mysteries of Mithra.* New York: Dover Publications, Inc., T323.

——, *Oriental Religions in Roman Paganism.* New York: Dover Publications, Inc., T321.

Festugière, A. J., *Personal Religion among the Greeks.* Berkeley, Calif.: University of California Press, CAL37.

Frankfort, H., *et al., Ancient Egyptian Religion: An Interpretation.* New York: Harper & Brothers, Harper Torchbooks, TB77.

——, *et al., Before Philosophy.* Baltimore: Penguin Books, Inc., A198.

——, *The Birth of Civilization in the Near East.* New York: Doubleday & Company, Inc., Anchor Books, A89.

Glover, T. R., *The Conflict of Religions in the Roman Empire.* Boston: Beacon Press, BP94.

Graves, Robert, *The Greek Myths* (2 vols.). Baltimore: Penguin Books, Inc., A1026-27.

Guthrie, W. K. C., *The Greeks and their Gods.* Boston: Beacon Press, BP2.

Harrison, Jane, *Prolegomena to the Study of Greek Religion.* Cleveland: The World Publishing Company, Meridian Books, MG3.

Hatch, Edwin, *The Influence of Greek Ideas on Christianity,* intro. by Frederick C. Grant. New York: Harper & Brothers, Harper Torchbooks, TB18.

Kraemer, Samuel Noah, *Sumerian Mythology.* New York: Harper & Brothers, Harper Torchbooks, TB18.

Murphy, Roland E., *The Dead Sea Scrolls and the Bible.* Westminster, Md.: The Newman Press, 1961.

Murray, Gilbert, *Five Stages of Greek Religion.* New York: Doubleday & Company, Inc., Anchor Books, A51.

Nilsson, Martin P., *Greek Folk Religion.* New York: Harper & Brothers, Harper Torchbooks, TB78.

Rose, H. J., *Gods and Heroes of the Greeks.* Cleveland: The World Publishing Company, Meridian Books, M59.

——, *Religion in Greece and Rome.* New York: Harper & Brothers, Harper Torchbooks, TB55.

Sauneron, Serge, *Priests of Ancient Egypt.* New York: (Evergreen Profile Book), Evergreen Books, Grove Press, Inc., P12.

Williams, Albert N., *What Archaeology Says about the Bible.* New York: Association Press, Reflection Books, 507.

Wilson, John A., *Culture of Ancient Egypt.* Chicago: University of Chicago Press, Phoenix Books, P11.

Wright, G. Ernest, ed., *Biblical Archaeology: Abr. Ed.* Philadelphia: Westminster Press, 20-0306.

CHAPTER FOUR: JUDAISM

EXTRABIBLICAL AND POSTBIBLICAL JEWISH WRITINGS

Baron, Salo W. and Joseph L. Blau, eds., *Judaism: Postbiblical and Talmudic Period.* Indianapolis, Ind.: The Liberal Arts Press Division of The Bobbs-Merrill Company, Inc., Library of Liberal Arts, LLA135.

Gaster, T. H., *The Dead Sea Scriptures in English Translation.* New York: Doubleday & Company, Inc., Anchor Books, A92.

Goldin, Judah, trans., *The Living Talmud: Wisdom of the Fathers and Its Classical Commentaries.* New York: New American Library of World Literature, Inc., Mentor Books, MT286.

Herford, R. Travers, *The Ethics of the Talmud: Sayings of the Fathers.* New York: Schocken Books, Inc., SB23.

Josephus, Flavius, *The Great Roman-Jewish War with the Life of Josephus,* intro. by William R. Farmer. New York: Harper & Brothers, Harper Torchbooks, TB74.

———, *The Jewish War,* trans., G. A. Williamson. Baltimore: Penguin Books, Inc., L90.

———, *Jerusalem and Rome: The Writings of Josephus,* sel. and intro. by Nahum N. Glatzer. Cleveland: The World Publishing Company, Meridian Books, M106.

Runes, D. D., ed., *The Wisdom of the Kabbalah.* New York: Philosophical Library, Inc., Wisdom Library Paperbacks, 17.

Spinoza, Baruch, *Selections,* ed., John Wild. New York: Charles Scribner's Sons, 1961.

———, *On the Improvement of the Understanding,* trans. with intro. by Joseph Katz. Indianapolis, Ind.: The Liberal Arts Press Division of The Bobbs-Merrill Company, Inc., Library of Liberal Arts, LLA26.

Thomas, D. Winton, ed., *Documents from Old Testament Times.* New York: Harper & Brothers, Harper Torchbooks, TB85.

The Talmud of Jerusalem, intro. by D. D. Runes, Philosophical Library, Inc., Wisdom Library Paperbacks, 2.

HISTORY AND RELIGION OF JUDAISM

Abrahams, Israel, *Jewish Life in the Middle Ages.* Cleveland: The World Publishing Company, Meridian Books, JP4.

Adler, Joshua, *Philosophy of Judaism.* New York: Philosophical Library, Inc., Wisdom Library Paperbacks, 56.

Allegro, J. M., *The Dead Sea Scrolls.* Baltimore: Penguin Books, Inc., A376.

Baab, Otto J., *The Theology of the Old Testament.* Nashville, Tenn.: Abingdon Press, Apex Books, E1.

Baeck, Leo, *The Essence of Judaism*. New York: Schocken Books, Inc., SB6.

Belford, Lee, *Introduction to Judaism*. New York: Association Press, Reflection Books, 545.

Bentwich, Norman, *The Jews in Our Time*. Baltimore: Penguin Books, Inc., A468.

Buber, Martin, *Moses: The Revelation and the Covenant*. New York: Harper & Brothers, Harper Torchbooks, TB27.

———, *The Way of Man According to the Teachings of Hasidism*. Wallingford, Pa.: Pendle Hill Pamphlets, 1960.

Cornhill, C. H., *History of the People of Israel*, trans. W. H. Carruth. La Salle, Ind.: The Open Court Publishing Co., P26.

Driver, S. R., *An Introduction to the Literature of the Old Testament*. Cleveland: The World Publishing Company, Meridian Books, MG29.

Epstein, Isidore, *Judaism*. Baltimore: Penguin Books, Inc., A440.

Freud, Sigmund, *Moses and Monotheism*. New York: Random House, Inc., Vintage Books, Inc., V14.

Gaster, Theodor H., *Passover: Its History and Tradition*. Boston: Beacon Press, LR16.

Glazer, Nathan, *American Judaism*. Chicago: University of Chicago Press, The Chicago History of American Civilization Series.

Goodman, Paul, *History of the Jews,* rev. and enl. by Israel Cohen; intro. by Abba Hillel Silver. New York: E. P. Dutton & Co., Inc., Dutton Everyman Paperbacks, D33.

Harrison, R. K., *The Dead Sea Scrolls: An Introduction*. New York: Harper & Brothers, Harper Torchbooks, TB84.

Hay, Malcolm, *Europe and the Jews: The Pressure of Christendom on the People of Israel for 1900 Years*. Boston: Beacon Press, BP95.

Herberg, Will, *Judaism and Modern Man*. Cleveland: The World Publishing Company, Meridian Books, JP10.

Herford, R. Travers, *The Pharisees*. Boston: Beacon Press, BP134.

Husik, Isaac, *History of Mediaeval Jewish Philosophy*. Cleveland: The World Publishing Company, Meridian Books, 38-3533.

Ilton, Paul and MacLennan Roberts, *Moses and the Ten Commandments*. New York: Dell Publishing Co., B-108.

Lewy, Hans, Alexander Altmann, and Isaac Heinemann, eds., *Three Jewish Philosophers: Philo, Saadya Gaon, Jehuda Halevi*. Cleveland: The World Publishing Company, Meridian Books, JP13.

Marcus, Jacob R., *The Jew in the Medieval World*. Cleveland: The World Publishing Company, Meridian Books, JP14.

Margolis, Max and Alexander Marx, *History of the Jewish People*. Cleveland: The World Publishing Company, Meridian Books, JP6.

Neher, Andre, *Moses and the Vocation of the Jewish People*. New York: Harper & Brothers, Men of Wisdom Series, 7.

Oesterley, W. O. E. and Theodore H. Robinson, *Introduction to the Books of the Old Testament.* Cleveland: The World Publishing Company, Meridian Books, LA23.

Schechter, Solomon, *Studies in Judaism.* Cleveland: The World Publishing Company, Meridian Books, JP5.

Scholem, Gershom G., *Major Trends in Jewish Mysticism.* New York: Schocken Books, Inc., SB5.

Schürer, Emil, *A History of the Jewish People in the Time of Jesus,* abr. New York: Schocken Books, Inc., SB8.

Silver, Abba Hillel, *History of Messianic Speculation in Israel: From the First through the Seventeenth Centuries.* Boston: Beacon Press, BP80.

Smith, W. Robertson, *The Religion of the Semites.* Cleveland: The World Publishing Company, Meridian Books, ML4.

Strack, Hermann L., *Introduction to the Talmud and Midrash.* Cleveland: The World Publishing Company, Meridian Books, JP8.

Thackeray, H. St. John, *Josephus: The Man and the Historian.* New York: University Publishers, Inc., 1961.

Wellhausen, Julius, *Prolegomena to the History of Ancient Israel.* Cleveland: The World Publishing Company, Meridian Books, MG35.

Wilson, Edmund, *The Scrolls from the Dead Sea.* Cleveland: The World Publishing Company, Meridian Books, M69.

Wolfson, Harry Austryn, *Philosophy of Spinoza.* Cleveland: The World Publishing Company, Meridian Books, MG16.

Chapter Five: Zoroastrianism

SCRIPTURES

Ballou, Robert O., ed., *The Portable World Bible.* New York: The Viking Press, Inc., Paperbound Portables, P5.

Bouquet, A. C., *Sacred Books of the World.* Baltimore: Penguin Books, A283.

Browne, Lewis, *The World's Great Scriptures.* New York: The Macmillan Company, 54.

INTERPRETATION

Bouquet, A. C., *Comparative Religion.* Baltimore: Penguin Books, A89.

Braden, Charles S., *The World's Religions,* rev. Nashville, Tenn.: Abingdon Press, Apex Books, C1.

Ceadel, Eric B., ed., *Literatures of the East: A Survey.* New York: Grove Press, Inc., Evergreen Books, E167.

Gaer, Joseph, *How the Great Religions Began,* rev. ed. New York: New American Library of World Literature, Inc., Signet Key Books, KD359.

Kramer, Samuel Noah, *Mythologies of the Ancient World.* New York: Doubleday & Company, Inc., Anchor Books, A229.

Lewis, John, *Religions of the World Made Simple*. Garden City, N.Y.: Doubleday & Company, Inc., Made Simple Books, MS27.

CHAPTER SIX: CHRISTIANITY

BIBLICAL AND POSTBIBLICAL CHRISTIAN WRITINGS

Anselm, Saint. *Proslogium, Monologium: An Appendix in Behalf of the Fool by Gaunilon; and Cur Deus Homo*, trans. Sidney N. Deane; new intro. by Charles Hartshorne. La Salle, Ind.: The Open Court Publishing Co., P54.

Aquinas, Saint Thomas, *The Pocket Aquinas*, ed., Vernon J. Bourke. New York: Washington Square Press, Inc., W575.

———, *On the Truth of the Catholic Faith (Summa Contra Gentiles)* ; *Book Two: Creation*. New York: Doubleday & Company, Inc., D27.

———, *On the Truth of the Catholic Faith (Summa Contra Gentiles)* ; *Book Three, parts 1 and 2, Providence*. New York: Doubleday & Company, Inc., D28a, D28b.

———, *On the Truth of the Catholic Faith (Summa Contra Gentiles)* ; *Book Four: Salvation*. New York: Doubleday & Company, Inc., D29.

Augustine, Saint, *Of True Religion*. Chicago: Henry Regnery Co., Gateway Editions, 6042.

———, *On the Two Cities: Selections from The City of God,* ed., F. W. Strothmann. New York: Frederick Ungar Publishing Co., M101.

Barrett, C. K., ed., *New Testament Background: Selected Documents*. New York: Harper & Brothers, Harper Torchbooks, TB86.

Barry, Colman J., ed., *Readings in Church History*. Westminster, Md.: The Newman Press, 59-14755.

Boehme, Jacob, *Personal Christianity,* intro. and notes by Franz Hartmann. New York: Frederick Ungar Publishing Co., 502.

Calvin, John, *Institutes of the Christian Religion,* 2 vols. Grand Rapids, Mich.: Wm. B. Eerdmans Publishing Co., 1961.

———, *On God and Man,* ed. F. W. Strothmann. New York: Frederick Ungar Publishing Co., M103.

———, *On God and Political Duty,* intro. by John T. McNeill. Indianapolis, Ind.: The Liberal Arts Press Division of The Bobbs-Merrill Company, Inc., Library of Liberal Arts, LLA23.

Compact Bible. Pyramid Books, Pyramid Publications, Inc., PR10.

Fremantle, Anne, *The Papal Encyclicals in their Historical Context*. New York: New American Library of World Literature, Inc., Mentor Books, MT256.

Goodspeed, Edgar J., trans., *Apocrypha,* intro. by Moses Hadas. New York: Random House, Inc., Modern Library of the Worlds, 1959.

Kempis, Thomas à, *Of the Imitation of Christ,* trans. Abbot Justin McCann. New York: New American Library of World Literature, Inc., Mentor Books, MD193.

New Testament, Official Catholic Edition. New York: Doubleday & Company, Inc., Doubleday Image Book, D39.

Phillips, J. B., *The Gospels.* New York: The Macmillan Company, 49.

Williams, Michael, ed., *They Walked with God (The Book of Christian Classics)*, rev. and abr. Fawcett Publications, Inc., Premier Books, D60.

CHRISTIAN HISTORY AND THEOLOGY

Adam, Karl, *Roots of the Reformation.* New York: Sheed & Ward, Inc., 142A.

Anderson, Bernhard W., *The Unfolding Drama of the Bible.* New York: Association Press, Reflection Books, 510.

Bainton, Roland H., *Early Christianity.* Princeton, N.J.: D. Van Nostrand Company, Inc., Anvil Books, 49.

——, *Here I Stand.* Nashville, Tenn.: Abingdon Press, Apex Books, D1.

——, *Here I Stand: A Life of Martin Luther.* New York: New American Library of World Literature, Inc., MT310.

——, *The Reformation of the 16th Century.* Boston: Beacon Press, BP22.

Barth, Karl, *The Word of God and Word of Man,* trans. Douglas Horton. New York: Harper & Brothers, Harper Torchbooks, TB13.

Belloc, Hilaire, *Characters of the Reformation.* New York: Doubleday Image Books, D71.

——, *How the Reformation Happened.* New York: William Morrow and Company, Inc., Apollo Editions, Inc., A10.

Bowden, C. H., *A Short Dictionary of Catholicism.* New York: Philosophical Library, Inc., Wisdom Library Paperbacks, 3.

Bowie, Walter Russell, *The Master: A Life of Jesus Christ.* New York: Charles Scribner's Sons, SL14.

Branscomb, B. Harvie, *The Teachings of Jesus.* Nashville, Tenn.: Abingdon Press, Apex Books, B2.

Bright, John, *The Kingdom of God.* Nashville, Tenn.: Abingdon Press, Apex Books, A1.

Bultmann, Rudolf, *Jesus and the Word.* New York: Charles Scribner's Sons, SL16.

——, *Primitive Christianity in Its Contemporary Setting.* Cleveland: The World Publishing Company, Meridian Books, LA4.

Chéry, A., *What Is the Mass?* Westminster, Md.: The Newman Press, 1952.

Chesterton, G. K., *Saint Francis of Assisi.* New York: Doubleday Image Books, D50.

——, *Saint Thomas Aquinas,* New York: Doubleday Image Books, D36.

Clark, Elmer T., *The Small Sects in America,* rev. ed. Nashville, Tenn.: Abingdon Press, Apex Books, B3.

Cook, Stanley, *Introduction to the Bible.* Baltimore: Penguin Books, Inc., A144.

Corbett, James A., *The Papacy: A Brief History.* Princeton, N.J.: D. Van Nostrand Co., Inc., Anvil Books, 12.

Craig, Clarence Tucker, *The Beginning of Christianity*. Nashville, Tenn.: Abingdon Press, Apex Books, E2.

Cullmann, Oscar, *Peter*. Cleveland: The World Publishing Company, Meridian Books, LA21.

Daniel-Rops, Henri, *Jesus and His Times*, 2 vols. New York: Doubleday Image Books, D67a, D67b.

———, *This Is the Mass*. New York: Doubleday Image Books, D90.

D'Arcy, Martin, E. Gilson, *et al.*, *Saint Augustine*. Cleveland: The World Publishing Company, Meridian Books, M51.

Deissmann, Adolf, *Paul: A Study in Social and Religious History*. New York: Harper & Brothers, Harper Torchbooks, TB15.

Dillenberger, John D., and Claude Welch, *Protestant Christianity*. New York: Charles Scribner's Sons, SL17.

Dodd, C. H., *The Authority of the Bible*. New York: Harper & Brothers, Harper Torchbooks, TB43.

———, *The Bible Today*. New York: Cambridge University Press, 1960.

———, *The Meaning of Paul for Today*. Cleveland: The World Publishing Company, Meridian Books, LA8.

Drewes, C. F., *Introduction to the Books of the Bible*. St. Louis, Mo.: Concordia Publishing House, 12-2210.

Ellis, John Tracy, *American Catholicism*. Chicago: University of Chicago Press, The Chicago History of American Civilization Series, 1956.

Enslin, Morton S., *Christian Beginnings*. New York: Harper and Brothers, Harper Torchbooks, TB5.

———, *The Literature of the Christian Movement* (Conclusion of Christian Beginnings). New York: Harper & Brothers, Harper Torchbooks, TB6.

Feuerbach, Ludwig, *Essence of Christianity*, abr., E. Graham Waring, ed. New York: Frederick Ungar Publishing Company, M109.

Fosdick, Harry Emerson, *A Guide to Understanding the Bible*. New York: Harper & Brothers, Harper Torchbooks, TB2.

Fouard, Constant, *Life of Christ*. New York: Golden Press, Inc., 1152.

Fremantle, Anne, *Treasury of Early Christianity*. New York: New American Library of World Literature, Inc., MT285.

Goguel, Maurice, *Jesus and the Origins of Christianity*, intro. by C. Leslie Mitton, vol. 1, *Prolegomena to the Life of Jesus;* Vol. 2, *The Life of Jesus*. New York: Harper & Brothers, Harper Torchbooks, TB65, TB66.

Goodspeed, Edgar J., *How Came the Bible*. Nashville, Tenn.: Abingdon Press, Apex Books, A4.

———, *The Life of Jesus*. New York: Harper & Brothers, Harper Torchbooks, TB1.

———, *Paul*. Nashville, Tenn.: Abingdon Press, Apex Books, D2.

Grant, Frederick C., *An Introduction to New Testament Thought*. Nashville, Tenn.: Abingdon Press, Apex Books, A5.

Hardon, John A., *The Protestant Churches of America*. Westminister, Md.: The Newman Press, 1958.

Harnack, Adolf, *Outlines of the History of Dogma,* intro. by Philip Rieft. Boston: Beacon Press, BP49.

——, *What Is Christianity?,* intro. by Rudolf Bultmann. New York: Harper & Brothers, Harper Torchbooks, TB17.

Harrison, Martin, *Credo: A Practical Guide to the Catholic Faith,* abr. New York: Golden Press, Inc., 1957.

Herberg, Will, *Protestant, Catholic, Jew,* rev. ed. New York: Doubleday & Company, Inc., Anchor Books, A195.

Holl, Karl, *The Cultural Significance of the Reformation.* Cleveland: The World Publishing Company, Meridian Books, LA25.

Hughes, Phillip, *Popular History of the Catholic Church.* New York: Doubleday Image Books, D4.

——, *Popular History of the Reformation.* New York: Doubleday Image Books, D92.

Inge, W. R., *Christian Mysticism.* Cleveland: The World Publishing Company, Meridian Books, LA3.

Klausner, Joseph, *From Jesus to Paul,* trans. William P. Stinespring. Boston: Beacon Press, BP115.

Knox, Ronald, *Belief of Catholics.* New York: Doubleday Image Books, D72.

Lingle, Walter L., *Presbyterians: Their History and Beliefs,* rev. ed. Richmond, Va.: John Knox Press, 1960.

Ludwig, Emil, *Son of Man: The Story of Jesus,* rev. by author. New York: Fawcett Publications, Inc., Premier Books, D55.

Manschreck, Clyde L., *The Reformation and Protestantism Today.* Association Press, Reflection Books, 533.

Maritain, Jacques, *Saint Thomas Aquinas,* new trans.; rev. ed. Cleveland: The World Publishing Company, Meridian Books.

Marrou, Henri, *Saint Augustine and His Influence through the Ages.* New York: Harper & Brothers, Men of Wisdom Series, 2.

Marty, Martin E., *A Short History of Christianity.* Cleveland: The World Publishing Company, Meridian Books, LA24.

Maynard, Theodore, *The Story of American Catholicism,* 2 vols. vol. I. New York: Doubleday Image Books, D106 A, D106 B.

Nichols, James H., *A Short Primer for Protestants,* abr. New York: Association Press, Reflection Books, 503.

Niebuhr, H. Richard, *Christ and Culture.* New York: Harper & Brothers, Harper Torchbooks, TB3.

Packer, James, *"Fundamentalism" and the Word of God.* Grand Rapids, Mich.: William B. Eerdmans Publishing Co., 1958.

Papini, Giovanni, *Life of Christ,* Dorothy Canfield Fisher, tr. New York: Dell Publishing Co., Inc., 4780.

Renan, Ernest, *Life of Jesus.* New York: Dolphin Books, C59.

Rowley, H. H., *The Unity of the Bible.* Cleveland: The World Publishing Co., Meridian Books, LA16.

Sandmel, Samuel, *A Jewish Understanding of the New Testament.* New York: University Publishers, Inc., 1957.

Schmidt, Albert-Marie, *John Calvin.* New York: Harper & Brothers, Men of Wisdom Series, 10.

Schweitzer, Albert, *The Quest of the Historical Jesus.* New York: Macmillan Paperbacks, The Macmillan Company, 55.

Sohm, Rudolf, *Outlines of Church History.* Boston: Beacon Press, BP71.

Steinmann, Jean, *St. John the Baptist and the Desert Tradition.* New York: Harper & Brothers, Men of Wisdom Series, 5.

Tresmontant, Claude, *St. Paul and the Mystery of Christ.* New York: Harper & Brothers, Men of Wisdom Series, 1.

Troeltsch, Ernst, *The Social Teachings of the Christian Churches,* 2 vols., Vol. I and Vol. II. New York: Harper & Brothers, Harper Torchbooks, TB71, TB72.

Van Doornik N. G. M., *et al., Handbook of the Catholic Faith,* ed. John Greenwood. New York: Doubleday Image Books, D38.

Van Loon, Hendrik Willem, *The Story of the Bible.* New York: Pocket Books, Inc., Permabooks, M5005.

Walker, Reginald F., *Outline History of the Catholic Church,* 2 vols. Westminster, Md.: The Newman Press, 1951.

Walsh, John J., *This is Catholicism.* New York: Doubleday Image Books, D80.

Walsh, William Thomas, *Saint Peter the Apostle.* New York: Doubleday Image Books, D85.

Weiss, Johannes, *Earliest Christianity: A History of the Period* A.D. *30-150,* intro. by Frederick C. Grant, 2 vols. New York: Harper & Brothers, Harper Torchbooks, TB53, TB54.

Whale, J. S., *The Protestant Tradition.* New York: Cambridge University Press, 1959.

Williams, Michael, ed., *They Walked with God (The Book of Christian Classics),* newly rev. and abr. New York: Fawcett Publications, Inc., Premier Books, D60.

Wright, G. Ernest, and Reginald H. Fuller, *The Book of the Acts of God.* New York: Doubleday & Company, Inc., Anchor Books, A222.

CHAPTER SEVEN: ISLAM

THE QUR'AN AND EARLY MUSLIM WRITINGS

Dawood, N. J. tr., *The Koran.* Baltimore: Penguin Books, Inc., L52.

Jeffery, Arthur, ed., *Islam: Muhammad and His Religion.* Indianapolis, Ind.: The Liberal Arts Press Division of The Bobbs-Merrill Company, Inc., Library of Liberal Arts, LLA137.

Pickthall, Mohammed Marmaduke, (tr.), *The Meaning of the Glorious Koran.* Indianapolis, Ind.: New American Library of World Literature, Division of The Bobbs-Merrill Company, Inc., Library of Liberal Arts, MG375.

MUSLIM HISTORY AND THEOLOGY

Andrae, Tor, *Mohammed: The Man and His Faith*. New York: Harper & Brothers, Harper Torchbooks, TB62.

Atiyah, Edward, *The Arabs*. Baltimore: Penguin Books, Inc., A350.

Brockelmann, Carl, *History of the Islamic Peoples*. New York: G. P. Putnam's Sons, Capricorn Books, 204

Dermenghem, Emile, *Muhammad and the Islamic Tradition*. New York: Harper & Brothers, Men of Wisdom Series, 6.

Gibb, Hamilton A. R., *Mohammedanism*. New York: Oxford University Press, Inc., Galaxy Books, 90.

Guillaume, Alfred, *Islam*. New York: Penguin Books, Inc., A311.

Hitti, Philip K., *The Arabs—A Short History*. Chicago: Henry Regnery Company, Gateway Editions, 6033.

Kirk, George E., *A Short History of the Middle East: From the Rise of Islam to Modern Times*. New York: Frederick A. Praeger, Inc., U-501.

Lewis, Bernard, *The Arabs in History*. New York: Harper & Brothers, Harper Torchbooks, TB1029.

Pirenne, Henri, *Mohammed and Charlemagne*. Cleveland: The World Publishing Company, Meridian Books, M42.

Smith, Wilfred Cantwell, *Islam in Modern History*. New York: New American Library of World Literature, Inc., MD268.

Wheeler, G., *Racial Problems in Soviet Muslim Asia,* 2nd ed. New York: Oxford University Press, Inc., 1960.

Wilson, J. Christy, *Introducing Islam*. New York: Friendship Press, no. 111.

CHAPTER EIGHT: THE LAND OF INDIA

Basham, Arthur L., *The Wonder that Was India*. Evergreen Encyclopedia Number 1, New York: Grove Press, Inc., Evergreen Books, E145.

Brown, D. Mackenzie, *The White Umbrella: Indian Political Thought from Manu to Gandhi*. Berkeley, Calif.: University of California Press, Cal12.

Dasgupta, S. N., *Indian Idealism*. New York: Cambridge University Press.

Garbe, Richard, *India and Christendom,* trans. Lydia G. Robinson. LaSalle, Ill., The Open Court Publishing Co.

Schweitzer, Albert, *Indian Thought and Its Development*. Boston: Beacon Press, PB37.

Wallbank, T. Walter, *A Short History of India and Pakistan* (India in the New Era); rev. ed., abr. New York: New American Library of World Literature, Inc., Mentor Books, MD224.

Zimmer, Heinrich, *Philosophies of India*. Cleveland: The World Publishing Company, Meridian Books, MG6.

——, *Myths and Symbols of Indian Art and Civilization*. New York: Harper & Brothers, Harper Torchbooks, TR2005.

CHAPTER NINE: HINDUISM

EARLY HINDU WRITINGS

Isherwood, Christopher and Swami Prabhavananda, *The Song of God: Bhaga-vad-Gita*. New York: New American Library of World Literature, Inc., Mentor Books, MD103.

Kalidasa, *Shakuntala and Other Writings*, trans. Arthur W. Ryder. New York: E. P. Dutton & Co., Inc., Dutton Everyman Paperbacks, D40.

Prabhavananda, Swami and Frederick Manchester, trans., *The Upanishads*. New York: New American Library of World Literature, Inc., Mentor Books, MP386.

HINDU HISTORY AND RELIGION

Archer, W. G., *The Loves of Krishna*. New York: Grove Press, Inc., Evergreen Books, E124.

Bahm, Archie J., *Yoga: Union with the Ultimate*. New York: Frederick Ungar Publishing Company, 511.

Behanan, Kovoor T., *Yoga*. New York: Dover Publications, Inc., 1960.

Coomaraswamy, A. K., *The Dance of Shiva*, rev. ed. New York: The Noonday Press, N108.

———, *Hinduism and Buddhism*. New York: Philosophical Library, Inc., Wisdom Library Paperbacks, 52-WL.

Dasgupta, S. N., *Hindu Mysticism*. New York: Frederick Ungar Publishing Company, 501.

Guenon, Réné, *Man and His Becoming according to the Vedanta*. New York: The Noonday Press, N129.

Isherwood, Christopher, ed., *Vedanta for the Western World*. New York: The Viking Press, Inc., Compass Books, C64.

Pitt, Malcolm, *Introducing Hinduism*. New York: Friendship Press, no. 110.

Radhakrishnan, S., *The Hindu View of Life*. New York: The Macmillan Company, MP103.

Sen, K. M., *Hinduism*. Baltimore: Penguin Books, Inc., A515.

Wood, Ernest, *Yoga*. Baltimore: Penguin Books, Inc., A448.

CHAPTER TEN: JAINISM

SCRIPTURES

Bouquet, A. C., *Sacred Books of the World*. Baltimore: Penguin Books, Inc., A283.

Champion, Selwyn Gurney and Dorothy Short, *Readings from World Religions*. New York: Fawcett Publications, Inc., Premier Books, D85.

INTERPRETATION

Basham, Arthur L., *The Wonder That Was India*. New York: Evergreen Encyclopedia Number 1, Grove Press, Inc., Evergreen Books, E145.

Gaer, Joseph, *How the Great Religions Began,* rev. ed. New York: New American Library of World Literature, Inc., Signet Key Books, KD359.

CHAPTER ELEVEN: BUDDHISM

BUDDHIST WRITINGS

Bahm, Archie J., *The Philosophy of the Buddha*. New York: Collier Books, AS195V.

Burtt, Edwin A., ed., *The Teachings of the Compassionate Buddha*. New York: New American Library of World Literature, Inc., Mentor Books, MP380.

Carus, Paul, *The Gospel of Buddha*. La Salle, Ill.: The Open Court Publishing Company, P14.

Conze, Edward, trans., *Buddhist Scriptures*. Baltimore: Penguin Books, Inc., L88.

Evans-Wentz, W. Y., ed., *The Tibetan Book of the Dead*. New York: Oxford University Press, Galaxy Books, 39.

Hamilton, Clarence H., ed., *Buddhism: A Religion of Infinite Compassion.* Indianapolis, Ind.: The Liberal Arts Press Division of the Bobbs-Merrill Company, Inc., Library of Liberal Arts, LLA133.

Huang Po, *The Zen Teaching of Huang Po: On the Transmission of Mind,* trans. John Blofeld. New York: E. P. Dutton & Co., Inc., Dutton Everyman Paperbacks, E171.

Suzuki, D. T., *A Manual of Zen Buddhism*. New York: Grove Press, Inc., Evergreen Books, E231.

Wu Ch'eng-en, *Monkey,* trans. Arthur Waley. New York: Grove Press, Inc., Evergreen Books, E112.

BUDDHIST HISTORY AND RELIGION

Arnold, Edwin, *The Light of Asia. The Life and Teaching of Gautama*. New York: Dolphin Books, C289.

Benoit, Hubert, *The Supreme Doctrine. Psychological Studies in Zen Thought,* intro. Aldous Huxley. New York: The Viking Press, Inc., Compass Books, C43.

Blyth, R. H., *Zen in English Literature and Oriental Classics*. New York: E. P. Dutton & Co., Inc., Dutton Everyman Paperbacks, D57.

Briggs, William, ed., *Zen Anthology*. New York: Grove Press, Inc., Evergreen Books, E289.

Carus, Paul, *Dharma*. La Salle, Ill.: The Open Court Publishing Company, P56.

Conze, Edward, *Buddhism: Its Essence and Development*. New York: Harper & Brothers, Harper Torchbooks, TB58.

Herold, A. Ferdinand, *The Life of Buddha* translated according to the legends of India. Rutland, Vt.: Charles E. Tuttle Co., 1954.

Humphreys, Christmas, *Buddhism*. Baltimore: Penguin Books, Inc., A228.

———, *Zen Buddhism*. New York: The Macmillan Company, MP104.

King, Winston L., *In the Hope of Nibbana: The Ethics of Theravada Buddhism*. La Salle, Ill.: The Open Court Publishing Company, P93.

Latourette, Kenneth Scott, *Introducing Buddhism*. New York: Friendship Press, no. 109.

Linssen, Robert, *Living Zen*. New York: Grove Press, Inc., Evergreen Books, E203.

Malalasekera, G. P., and K. N. Jayatilleke, *Buddhism and the Race Question*. New York: Columbia University Press, International Documents Service, 1958.

Percheron, Maurice, *Buddha and Buddhism*. New York: Harper & Brothers, Men of Wisdom Series, 3.

Reps, Paul, ed., *Zen Flesh, Zen Bones*. New York: Doubleday & Company, Inc., Anchor Books, A233.

Senzaki, Nyogen and R. S. McCandless, trans., ed. *Buddhism and Zen*. New York: Philosophical Library, Inc., Wisdom Library Paperbacks, 6-WL.

Suzuki, D. T., *Essays in Zen Buddhism*. New York: Grove Press, Inc., Evergreen Books, E309.

———, *Zen Buddhism*, ed. William Barrett. New York: Doubleday & Company, Inc., Anchor Books, A90.

Watts, Alan W., *Beat Zen, Square Zen & Zen*. San Francisco: City Lights Books.

———, *Spirit of Zen: A Way of Life, Work and Art in the Far East*. New York: Grove Press, Inc., Evergreen Books, E219.

———, *Supreme Identity*. New York: The Noonday Press, N113.

———, *Way of Zen*. New York: New American Library of World Literature, Inc., Mentor Books, MD273.

CHAPTER TWELVE: SIKHISM

SCRIPTURES

Bouquet, A. C., *Sacred Books of the World*. Baltimore: Penguin Books, Inc., A283.

Champion, Selwyn Gurney and Dorothy Short, *Readings from World Religions*. New York: Fawcett Publications, Inc., Premier Books, D85.

INTERPRETATION

Gaer, Joseph, *How the Great Religions Began*. New York: New American Library of World Literature, Inc., Signet Books, KD359.

CHAPTER THIRTEEN: ORIGINS OF CHINESE RELIGION

Creel, H. G., *Chinese Thought: From Confucius to Mao Tse-Tung*. New York: New American Library of World Literature, Inc., Mentor Books, MD269.

Day, Clarence Burton, *The Philosophers of China*. New York: The Citadel Press.

Fairservis, Walter A., Jr., *Origins of Oriental Civilization*. New York: New American Library of World Literature, Inc., Mentor Books, MD251.

Fung-Yu-Lan, *A Short History of Chinese Philosophy*, ed. Derk Bodde. New York: The Macmillan Company, 22.

Giles, Herbert A., *A History of Chinese Literature*. New York: Grove Press, Inc., Evergreen Books, E118.

Granet, Marcel, *Chinese Civilization*. Cleveland: The World Publishing Company, Meridian Books, MG14.

Grousset, René, *The Rise and Splendour of the Chinese Empire*. Berkeley, Calif.: University of California Press, cal19.

Waley, Arthur, *Three Ways of Thought in Ancient China*. New York: Doubleday & Company, Inc., Anchor Books, A75.

Chapter Fourteen: Taoism

EARLY TAOIST WRITINGS

Lao Tze, *The Way of Life: Tao Te Ching*, trans. R. B. Blakney. New York: New American Library of World Literature, Inc., Mentor Books, M129.

——, *The Canon of Reason and Virtue (Tao Teh King)*, trans. Paul Carus. La Salle, Ill.: The Open Court Publishing Co., P55.

——, *Treatise on Response and Retribution (Ta'i-Shang Kan-Ying P'ien)*, trans. Teitaro Suzuki and Paul Carus. La Salle, Ill.: The Open Court Publishing Co., P64.

Waley, Arthur, *The Way and Its Power*. Grove Press, Inc., Evergreen Books, E84.

INTERPRETATION

Herbert, Edward, *A Taoist Notebook*. New York: Grove Press, Inc., Evergreen Books, WP2.

Chapter Fifteen: Confucianism

EARLY CONFUCIAN WRITINGS

Confucius, *The Living Thoughts of Confucius*, presented by Alfred Doeblin. New York: Fawcett Publications, Inc., Premier Books, D74.

Giles, Lionel, *The Sayings of Confucius*. New York: Grove Press, Inc., Evergreen Books, WP1.

Waley, Arthur, trans., *The Book of Songs*. New York: Grove Press, Inc., Evergreen Books, E209.

——, *The Analects of Confucius*. New York: Random House, Modern Library Paperback, P66.

Ware, James R., trans., *The Sayings of Confucius*. New York: New American Library of World Literature, Inc., Mentor Books, MD307.

———, *Sayings of Mencius*. New York: New American Library of World Literature, Inc., Mentor Books, MD307.

INTERPRETATION

Creel, H. G., *Confucius and the Chinese Way*. New York: Harper & Brothers, Harper Torchbooks, TB63.

Herbert, Edward, *A Confucian Notebook*. New York: Grove Press, Inc., Evergreen Books, WP5.

CHAPTER SIXTEEN: SHINTO

SCRIPTURES

Bouquet, A. C., *Sacred Books of the World*. Baltimore: Penguin Books, Inc., A283.

Champion, Selwyn Gurney and Dorothy Short, *Readings from World Religions*. New York: Fawcett Publications, Inc., Premier Books, D85.

Keene, Donald, ed., *Anthology of Japanese Literature: Earliest Era to Mid-Nineteenth Century*. New York: Grove Press, Inc., Evergreen Books, E216.

———, *Japanese Literature: An Introduction for Western Readers*. Grove Press, Inc., Evergreen Books, E9.

INTERPRETATION

Bouquet, A. C., *Comparative Religion*. Baltimore: Penguin Books, Inc., A89.

Bunce, William K., ed., *Religions in Japan*. Rutland, Vt.: Charles E. Tuttle Co., 1955.

Ceadel, Eric B., ed., *Literatures of the East: A Survey*. New York: Grove Press, Inc., Evergreen Books, E167.

Gaer, Joseph, *How the Great Religions Began*. New York: New American Library of World Literature, Inc., Signet Books, KD359.

Kramer, Samuel Noah, *Mythologies of the Ancient World*. New York: Doubleday & Company, Inc., Anchor Books, A229.

Parrinder, E. G., *Introduction to Asian Religions*. Seraph Books, Seabury Press.

Ross, Floyd H. and Tynette Hill, *Great Religions by Which Men Live. (Questions That Matter Most Asked by the World's Great Religions)*. New York: Fawcett Publications, Inc., Premier Books, D120.

INDEX

A

Adi Granth, 128
ahimsa, 106
Ahura Mazdah, 39-44
Ainu, 150
ajiva, 104-6
Allah, 71-75
Amaterasu, 152
Amesha Spentas, 41
Amitabha, 123
Amos, 29
Ancestor worship:
  Chinese, 133
  Confucian, 147
  primitive, 18
  Shinto, 152
  Vedic, 88
Angad, 129
Angra Mainyu, 40-43
Animism, 15
Apocalyptic thought, 47
Apocrypha, 30
Arhat, 115
Arjun, 128-9
Aryans, 85-86
Atharva Veda, 86
Atman, 90
avidya, 113

B

Baal, 27, 28
Babylonians, 29
Bhagavad-Gita, 95-96, 99
Bhakti-marga, 98-99
Biblical religions:
  classified, 10
  common elements in, 22-23
Bodhi, 110
Bodhisattva, 117, 119-123
Bøn religion, 118
Brahma, god, 91, 125
Brahman, 90
Brahmanas, 89

Buddhism:
  classified, 10
  dhamma, 119
  four noble truths, 111-112
  Hinayana sect, 116
  Hindu heresy, 94
  Mahayana sect, 116-123
  missionary dynamics, 118-121
  sangha, 119
  scriptures, 110
  Theravada sect, 116
  three refuges, 115
  world view, 112-115
  world view, Mahayana, 121-123
Bushido ethics, 154

C

Caliphate, 77
Canaanites, 27, 28
Chang Tao-Ling, 139
Ch'ih, 148
Ch'in dynasty, 147
Chinvat Bridge, 43
Chou dynasty, 131, 141
Christianity:
  classified, 10
  Eastern Church, 61-63
  missionary dynamics, 56-59
  Protestant Reformation, 64-65
  scriptures, 51-52
  world view, 52-55
Chuang Tzu, 135, 138
Ch'un Ch'iu, 143
Chün tze, 144-147
Chung Yung, 143
Codrington, Bishop, 9, 14
Conduct (*see each world view*)
  defined, 4
Confucianism:
  classified, 10
  four classes, 145
  scriptures, 142-144
  world view, 145-147
Confucius:
  life, 141-2

Confucius (*Cont.*)
name, 141
teachings, 145-7
Constantine, Emperor, 61
Cosmos (*see each world view*)
defined, 3

D

Daevas, 42
Dasam Granth, 128
Dead Sea Scrolls, 34, 44
Deity (*see each world view*)
defined, 3
Destiny (*see each world view*)
defined, 4
Devil, 35, 41, 49, 53, 71, 74
Dharma, 91, 113
Dharma-kaya, 122
dhyana, 139
Dhyani Buddhas, 122
Diaspora Judaism, 34
Digambara sect, 107
du Noüy, Lecomte, 6

E

Eastern Church (*see* Christianity)
Essenes, 33
Exodus, Hebrew, 26

F

Fetish, 15, 17, 153
Filial piety, 143, 144, 146
Five Doctrines of Islam, 70-72
Five Pillars of the Faith, 72-73
Four Noble Truths, 111-112
Frazer, Sir James G., 9
Freud, Sigmund, 9

G

Gautama, the Buddha:
as *Avatar* of Vishnu, 97
life, 108-110
teachings, 111-112
Ghetto, 37
Gobind Singh, 129-30
Guru, 126-130

H

Hajj, 73
Hari, 126-7
Haskalah (Jewish enlightenment), 37
Hebrew (*see* Judaism)
defined, 24
Hebrew Bible, 30
Hegira, 69
Hinduism:
classified, 10
four classes, 89
four ends of man, 89
four stages of life, 89
scriptures:
sectarian, 94-96
Upanishads, 90
Vedic, 86
six orthodox systems, 100-101
world view:
sectarian (popular), 96-100
Upanishadic, 91-93
Vedic, 86-88
Holy Spirit, Christian, 50, 53
Hsia dynasty, 131
Hsiao, 143, 144, 146, 153
Hsiao Ching, 143
Hsün Tze, 147

I

I Ching, 143
Islam:
Caliphate, 77
classified, 10
Five Doctrines, 70-72
Five Pillars, 72-73
four schools of law, 78
Kalima, or creed, 72
missionary dynamics, 75-76
scriptures, 69-71
Shiite sect, 78
Sufis, 78
Sunni sect, 78
Wahhabi order, 79
world view, 73-75
Israel, State of, 38
Israelites, 25
Izanagi, 152
Izanami, 152

J

Jainism:
classified, 10
Hindu heresy, 94
scriptures, 104
sects, 107
world view, 104-6
Jesus:
ethics of, 49
as Jewish Messiah, 50
life, 48-50
as Lord (*Kurios*), 51
resurrection of, 50
teachings, 48-50
Jews, defined, 25
Jimmu Tenno, 152
jivas, 104-6
Jnana-marga, 98
John the Baptist, 48
Josephus, Flavius, 31
Judaism:
classified, 10
Conservative Judaism, 38
German Nazi persecution, 37
Orthodox Judaism, 38
Persian dualism, 32
Reform Judaism, 38
scriptures:
Hebrew, 25-26
rabbinic, 31
theodicy, 32
world view:
pre-exilic, 27-29
rabbinic, 34-36
Judo, 140
Ju-jitsu, 140
Ju Chiao, 141, 148
Jung, Carl, 9

K

Ka'ba, 126
Kabbalah, 37
Kabir, 125
Kami, 150-154
Kami no michi, 150
Karma, 83, 92, 105, 111, 126
Karma-marga, 98
Kevala, 106
Khadijah, 67-68

Khalsa, 129
Kingdom of God:
in Christianity, 48, 49, 55
in Judaism, 32
Zoroastrian, 43-44
Kojiki, 151
Kismet, 71-72, 127
Kwan Yin, 120, 155

L

Lang, Andrew, 9
Lao Tzu, 131, 134
Laws of Manu, 95
Li, 144, 146, 148
Li-Chi, 143
London Buddhist Society, 124
Lun-Yü, 143, 144
Luther, Martin, 64-65

M

Mahabharata, 95
Mahavira:
life, 103-4
teachings, 104-6
Mahayana Buddhism, 140, 148, 154, 155, 156
Magic, 15
Maimonides, 36
Man (*see each world view*)
defined, 4, 7
man and society, 7
man and space, 6
man and time, 6
Mana, 9, 14-18
Manushi Buddhas, 122
Man's plight (*see each world view*)
defined, 4
Mao Tse-tung, 149
Mara, 109
Marcion, 60
Marett, R. R., 9
Maya, 91, 111, 126
Mecca, 67, 68, 69, 73, 126
Medicine man, 15
Medina, 69
Meiji reform, 155
Mencius, 143, 147
Meng Tze (*see* Mencius)
Messiah, 32, 47, 50

Micah, Hebrew prophet, 27
Middle Way, 112
Mishnah, 31, 33, 34, 35
Missionary religions:
  adaptability of, 55
  Buddhism, 118-121
  Christianity, 56-58
  continuity of, 55
  Islam, 75-77
  universality of, 55
Mohammed:
  life, 67-69
  message, 70-73
Moksha, 84, 103
Monotheistic religions (*see* Biblical religions)
Moses, 25, 26, 46
Müller, Max, 8

N

Nanak:
  life, 125-6
  teachings, 126-8
  world view, 126-7
Neo-Confucianism, 148
New Testament, 51-52
Nicene Creed, 60-61
Nihongi, 151
Nirmana-kaya, 122
Nirvana, 83, 94, 114, 117-118, 123

O

Om mane padme om, 122-123

P

Pahlavi texts, 40
Pali scriptures, 110, 116
Paramatman, 90
Parsis, 39, 45 (*see also* Zoroastrianism)
Prakriti, 113
Punar-janman, 91
Puranas, 96
Purushas, 111
Paul, the apostle:
  letters of, 52
  quoted, 57
Persian Empire, 29, 44

Peter, 59
Philo Judaeus, 31
Pope (Papacy), 61, 62, 64
Primitive religion:
  classified, 10
  locations, 12, 13
  world view, 16-18
Protestant Reformation (*see* Christianity)
Pseudepigrapha, 31, 44

Q

Quran, 69-71, 126

R

Rabbis, 33
Ram Das, 129
Ramakrishna, 102
Ramanaju, 90, 100
Ramayana, 95
Religion:
  defined, 7
  origins, 8
Religions:
  classified, 10
  numbers of followers, 10
Rig Veda, 86
Roy, Ram Mohan, 102
Ryobu Shinto, 155

S

Sadducees, 33
Salvation (*see each world view*)
  defined, 4
Sama Veda, 86
Sambhoga-kaya, 122
Samsara, 83, 94
Sangha, 104, 114
Sarasvati, Swami Dayanand, 102
Sat Nam, 126-127
Satori, 140
Schmidt, Wilhelm, 9
Shakti, 97
Shang dynasty, 131
Shang-Ti, 145
Shaoshyant, 42
Shema (Jewish), 28
Shankara, 90, 100

Shi-Huang-Ti, Emperor, 142, 147
Shih Ching, 143
Shinto:
  classified, 10
  Ryobu, or Dual *Shinto,* 155
  scriptures, 151
  Sect Shinto, 155
  Shrine Shinto, 155
  State Shinto, 155
  world view, 151-154
Shiva, 97
Shu, 144, 146, 154
Shu Ching, 143
Siddhartha (*see* Gautama)
Sikhism:
  classified, 10
  scriptures, 128
  world view, 126-127
Skandhas, 113
Ssu Shu (Four Books), 142, 143
Sun Yat Sen, 149
Susa-no-wo, 152
Svetambara sect, 107
Synagogue, 32

T

Tabu, 14, 15, 17
Ta Hsueh, 143
Taiping Rebellion, 139
Talmud, 31, 33, 34, 35, 36
Tanha, 113
Tao, 132, 134-140, 145, 150
Taoism:
  classified, 10
  scriptures, 134-135
  world view, 135-138
Tao Teh Ching, 134-138
Tat tvam asi, 92, 93
Three jewels of Jainism, 106
T'ien, 132, 145
Tirthankara, 107
Torah, 25
Tri-murti, 96, 121
Tripitaka, 110
Tylor, Sir Edward, 8

U

Upanishads, 90-93, 137

V

Vardhamana, 103
Vedas, the four, 86, 126
Vendidad, 40
Vishnu, 97, 100, 126

W

Wach, Joachim, 9
Waley, Arthur, 136, n.
World view:
  Buddhist:
    early, 112-114
    Mahayana, 121-123
  Christian, 52-55
  Confucian, 145-147
  defined, 3, 4
  Hindu:
    sectarian (popular), 96-100
    Upanishadic, 91-93
    Vedic, 87-88
  Islamic, 73-75
  Jainist, 104-6
  Judaic:
    pre-exilic, 27-29
    rabbinic, 34-36
  primitive, 16-18
  Shinto, 151-154
  Sikh, 126-127
  Taoist, 135-138
  Zoroastrian, 41-44
Wu-wei, 135
Wu Ching (Five Classics), 142

Y

Yahweh, 26, ff., 46, 51
Yajur Veda, 86
yang-yin, 132-133, 145, 151
Yashts, 40
Yasna, 40
Yengishiki, 151
Yoga, 91

Z

Zarathustra (*see* Zoroaster)
Zealots, 33

Zen Buddhism, 139-140
Zernov, Nicolas, 63
Zoroaster:
    life, 39-40
    teachings, 41-44

Zoroastrianism:
    classified, 10
    Persian dualism in Judaism, 32
    scriptures, 40
    world view, 41-43